STUDY WORKBOOK FOR ISBN 978-1933039787

Real Estate Closing Settlement Agent Training

Library of Congress -in-Publication Data
October 2012

Real Estate Settlement Agent Study Workbook for ISBN 978-1933039213

Printed in the United States of America

10 9 8 7 6 5 4 3 2 1

The enclosed material is designed for educational purposes only. Each State may have different certification and specific guidelines. Please refer to your State for additional and future information. The information contained herein is considered correct at the time of creation but laws and regulations are updated frequently and the reader assumes the responsibility for confirming current regulations and applicable data. The publisher and author make no warranty as to the success of the individuals using the training material contained herein. The publisher and author make no warranty as to any action taken by any individual completing this program. The reader is responsible for the appropriate use of the materials and information provided. This publication is designed to provide accurate and authoritative information concerning the subject matter. All material is sold with the understanding that neither the author nor the publisher guarantees the actions of any individual making use of the inclusions. Neither the author nor the publisher is rendering a legal opinion, accounting recommendation or other professional service. If legal advice or other expert assistance is desired, the services of a legal professional or other individual should be sought. The applicable federally released forms, disclosures and notices are generated from public domain. Copyright law does apply to all intellectual materials and all rights under said law are reserved b y the copyright owner.

Coursework is available at special quantity discounts to use as premiums and sales promotions within corporate or private training programs. To obtain information or inquire about availability please write to Director, PO Box 1, Hollidaysburg, PA 16648.

NOTICE

STUDY WORKBOOK FOR ISBN 978-1933039213

Real Estate Closing Settlement Agent Training

Flashcard Set

The flashcard set is designed to assist you in testing you retention of the fundamentals contained within the materials. You should complete the coursework and then use a file card to cover the second row that contains the answers to each question. Review the questions and then check your answers.

The included self-tests are designed to assist you in determining your mastery of each chapter of the course. When you feel you are ready for enhanced testing, complete the self-test segments of the workbook. Completing the self-tests without reference to the written text is the best method of assessing your knowledge base. If you are unable to answer a particular question, you should review the applicable chapter in its entirety.

It is a critical portion of your function at the meeting to _____ that all necessary _____ are obtained and to _____ these _____.

It is a critical portion of your function at the meeting to <u>confirm</u> that all necessary <u>signatures</u> are obtained and to <u>witness</u> these <u>signatures.</u>

What is a Settlement?

The time at which a property transfer is finalized.

What is the purpose of the laws that govern the ethics and disclosures with which you handle loan processes?

The laws and acts governing ethics and disclosure practices are in place to protect the interest of the public and make the obtainment of housing and home mortgage funds a fair practice for all applicants.

The _____ is the written declaration of a statement of _____ that is made voluntarily and sworn to or affirmed before some person legally _____ to administer an oath or affirmation.

The affidavit is the written declaration of a statement of fact that is made voluntarily and sworn to or affirmed before some person legally authorized to administer an oath or affirmation.

The severance of a resource right may be completed by

- Conveyance or grant
- A lease of the named rights
- Adverse possession
- All of the above

The severance of a resource right might be accomplished by conveyance or grant, a lease of the named rights, or adverse possession.

The escrow agent will use the _____ _____ as a _____ to the tasks that must be completed in order for the transaction to close.

The escrow agent will use the real estate purchase agreement as a guide to the tasks that must be completed in order for the transaction to close.

What is a settlement statement?

- HUD 1
- Statement that itemizes all closing costs payable at the closing
- Final analysis of all costs and credits applicable to the loan process
- All of the Above

A settlement statement, also termed a HUD 1 is a statement that itemizes all closing costs payable at the closing and defines the costs and credits applicable to the loan process.

What is Title Insurance?

The insurance policy that agrees to indemnify the insured against defects in the title.

The settlement agent will _____ ____ the _____ of all parties present at the meeting.

The settlement agent will <u>record</u> the <u>legal name</u> of all parties present at the meeting.

When must a right to cancel be provided?

- At the settlement meeting
- When a borrower refinances their primary residence
- When a borrower obtains a loan against their primary residence
- When a borrower refinances any property

A notice of the borrower's right to cancel must be provided in relationship to any credit transaction that involves a security interest in a borrower's primary residence.

What is Tenancy in Common?

A form of joint tenancy by two or more individuals or entities where each obtains an undivided interest in real property.

The settlement or escrow agent is a _____ third party selected by the _____ and the _____.

The settlement or escrow agent is a neutral third party selected by the buyer and the seller.

Improvements may include

- Pipelines
- Pavement
- Buildings
- All of the above

Improvements may include pipelines, pavement, and buildings on the land.

RESPA

- Helps consumers shop for settlement services
- Eliminates referral fees
- Requires specific borrower disclosures
- All of the above

RESPA helps consumers shop for settlement services, eliminates referral fees, and requires specific borrower disclosures

What is the Bundle of Rights?

All rights of ownership of real property. Synonym for estate.

Which of the following is not considered real property?

- A dresser
- Trees
- A fence
- None of the above

A dresser is an item of personal property and will not be included within the transfer of real property.

What is an acknowledgement?

A declaration made before a notary or other official certifying that the signing of a document is of a voluntary act undertaken of ones own free will.

The borrower has the right to cancel any credit transaction involving their home within 3 days of the funding of the transaction.

- True
- False

TRUE - The borrower has the right to cancel any credit transaction involving their home within 3 days of the funding of the transaction.

What is an abstract of title?

The chronological history of the most relevant parts of every recorded instrument regarding a title.

Limitations in the owner's rights may be imposed by

- Public Sources
- Private Sources
- Both public and private sources
- None of the above

Limitations in the owner's rights may be imposed by both public and private sources.

When must a right to cancel be provided?

• At the settlement meeting
• When a borrower refinances their primary residence
• When a borrower obtains a loan against their primary residence
• When a borrower refinances any property

A notice of the borrower's right to cancel must be provided in relationship to any credit transaction that involves a security interest in a borrower's primary residence.

What is an amendment?

A change made to correct an error or to alter an agreement.

Pre-paid items are dictated by

- the sales agreement
- underwriting guidelines
- available funds
- none of the above

Prepaid item requirements will be dictated by underwriting guidelines.

What is a Specific Lien?

A specific lien against a particular piece of property.

What are Closing Costs?

Expenses incurred by buyers and sellers in transferring ownership of a property. Closing costs normally include an origination fee, an attorney's fee, taxes, escrow payments, and charges for title insurance. Lenders or Real Estate Agents provide estimates of closing costs to prospective homebuyers.

Tenancy by Severalty means there

- Are 2 owners
- Are multiple Owners
- Is 1 Owner
- Any of the Above

Tenancy by Severalty means the property is owned by one owner.

Concurrent owners share

- The property
- Unity
- Ownership interest
- All of the Above

Concurrent owners share the property, unity and ownership interest in the property.

Any owner of a property may

- Incur liens
- Convey interest
- Create a condemnation
- All of the Above

Any owner of a property may incur liens, convey interest, or create a condemnation.

What type of lien is created against a property when an owner uses it as collateral to borrower money?

- General Lien
- Voluntary Lien
- Involuntary Lien
- All of the Above

A voluntary lien is created against a property when an owner uses it as collateral to borrower money.

The funding is when

- The underwriter completes a final loan review
- The monies borrowed are wired or sent to the closing agent
- The monies borrowed are disbursed to the proper individuals
- None of the Above

The funding is when the monies borrowed are wired or sent to the closing agent.

What is Disbursement?

The release of funds held in an escrow account.

A quitclaim deed

- contains no warranties
- contains no covenants
- does not promise the seller even holds interest in the property
- all of the above

A quitclaim deed contains no warranties, covenants, or even the promise that the individual signing the deed holds any interest in the property.

What is Closing?

The meeting at which the sale of a property is finalized. The buyer signs the lender agreement for the mortgage and pays' closing costs and escrow amounts. The buyer and seller sign documents to transfer the ownership of the property. Also known as the settlement.

A deed restriction may limit

- the action of a lender
- the action of the owner
- the action of an investor
- all of the above

A deed restriction may limit the actions of any party gaining ownership or other interest in a property.

What is the Good Faith Estimate?

A written estimate of closing costs that the lender must provide to prospective homebuyers within three days of submitting a mortgage loan application.

What does it mean to execute?

To validate a document.

What is an encumbrance?

Any item that affects the title to real property such as liens, easements, or deed restrictions.

What are Closing Costs?

Expenses incurred by buyers and sellers in transferring ownership of a property. Closing costs normally include an origination fee, an attorney's fee, taxes, escrow payments, and charges for title insurance. Lenders or Real Estate Agents provide estimates of closing costs to prospective homebuyers.

Section

2

Skill Enhancement Self-Tests

Name:
Settlement Agent Review Questions
Closing Overview
Score:
Instructor

1.   Title Closing is the time when a real estate transaction?

_____

_____

_____

_____

_____

2.   Other common terms used to describe title include:

_____

_____

_____

_____

_____

3.   What common forms of funds may the borrower bring to the closing?

_____

_____

_____

_____

_____

4.	It is the function of the settlement agent to?

_____

_____

_____

_____

_____

5.	Prorating is:

_____

_____

_____

_____

_____

1.   It is a critical portion of your function at the meeting to _____ that all necessary
        _____ are obtained and to _____ these

        _____

2.   During the closing, all matters negotiated in the sales agreement will be
        _____ and   confirmation that all _____ have been
        met will be made by both the buyer and the seller.

3.   The escrow agents task list should detail every _____ ,
        _____ ,   and applicable _____
        that must occur to reach the final legal _____ of the property.

4.   If the buyer or seller is unable to attend the closing or another individual expected to
        attend is unable to be present, a _____ will be
        _____.

5.   The parties to a transaction are _____ likely to meet if the closing is completed in the
        form of an _____.

6.   The most common forms of settlement are the _____

_____

_____

_____

_____

_____

7.   What is the primary component that defines a round table closing?

_____

_____

_____

_____

_____

8.   When you are proving settlement services for a transaction that contains a mortgage, the lender will often provide

_____

_____

_____

_____

_____

9.   A transaction cannot be considered finalized until

_____

_____

_____

_____

_____

10.   What is a power of attorney?

_____

_____

_____

_____

_____

11.   A round table closing dictates that all parties

Name:
Settlement Agent Review Questions
Chapter 2 – Party Obligations
Score:
Instructor

1.   The escrow agent will use the _____ as a

        _____ to the tasks that must be completed in order for the transaction
        to close.

2.   Escrow or settlement processes can typically be completed in

        _____.

3.   What are the three most common items the seller or seller's attorney is responsible for
        providing at the closing meeting?
        _____

        _____

        _____

        _____

        _____

        _____

4.   The buyer is responsible for having _____

        _____

        _____

        _____

        _____

        _____

5.   The lender will provide

_____

_____

_____

_____

_____

6.   What are the three most common items the lender will provide for a closing that uses
       mortgage funds?

_____

_____

_____

_____

_____

7.   Name the three most common tasks an escrow agent must complete at the closing
       table?

_____

_____

_____

_____

_____

8   An offset statement is

_____

_____

_____

_____

_____

9.   Prior to closing the settlement agent should contact each party and confirm

_____

_____

_____

_____

_____

10.   What are the most common tasks the settlement agent will perform at and
       immediately following the settlement meeting?

_____

_____

_____

_____

_____

1. A representative may have been _____ by one of the parties to _____ on their behalf at the settlement meeting.

2. The settlement agent will _____ the _____ of all parties   present at the meeting.

3. The escrow agent is a _____ third party selected by the _____ and the _____.

4. Most States require that the settlement agent obtain a _____ copy of _____   for each party who will be signing documents.

5. The mortgage lender will provide _____ of the required
   _____ and _____ that must be completed to secure the mortgage loan on the _____

6. If an existing loan is to be assumed by the buyer as part of the transaction, the escrow agent will obtain the _____ _____
   _____ and any _____ required by the buyer or the seller to complete the _____.

7. The settlement may also be termed
   _____
   _____
   _____
   _____
   _____
   _____

8. At a dry closing, the fund from the lender _____

_____

_____

_____

_____

_____

9. When will the funds from a dry closing be provided to the settlement agent? ___

_____

_____

_____

_____

10. What is included in the escrow instructions? _____

_____

_____

_____

_____

_____

1.   Commissions are _____ to be paid to _____
        _____ and must be noted at the opening of escrow and incorporated into the
        settlement statement.

2.   The _____ _____ will detail the specifics of any
        mortgages that must be _____ prior to the transfer of the property.

3.   The escrow agent will generate a transaction timeline based on the
        _____ detailed in the

        _____

4.   The firs task upon receipt of a new closing order is to _____

        _____

        _____

        _____

        _____

        _____

5.   Name the five most common items that the closing agent should note when a new
        closing order is received:

        _____

        _____

        _____

        _____

        _____

6. The financial specifics of a transaction of interest to the closing agent will include

_____

_____

_____

_____

_____

7. If a real estate agent is involved in the transaction, the two essential pieces of interest to the closing agent are

_____

_____

_____

_____

_____

8. The settlement agent will review the sales agreement to confirm

_____

_____

_____

_____

_____

9. Name the four most common parties that must review and approve property inspections before the closing can commence

_____

_____

_____

_____

_____

10.   The closing agent must obtain legal verification of _____

_____

_____

_____

_____

_____

Name:
Settlement Agent Review Questions
Chapter 5 – Potential Delays
Score:
Instructor

1.   The expected _____ for a real estate transaction will typically be
        included on the _____.

2.   If it becomes apparent that the agreed upon close date will not be met, an
        _____ to the _____
        must be created that _____   the closing date.

3.   If a contract cancellation occurs, the settlement agent must determine if there are
        _____   _____ outstanding and have the
        _____ who is deemed _____ for
        the cancellation or is detailed as the responsible party within the contracts make
        payment.

4.   The functions of the settlement agent will often be the _____
        items requiring _____in the transaction.

5.   The expected close date for the transaction will be based on _____

        _____

        _____

        _____

        _____

        _____

6.   What financial items must be considered when planning the flow of the settlement process?

_____

_____

_____

_____

_____

7.   What are the four most common affinity services that will affect the timeline of the closing?

_____

_____

_____

_____

_____

8.   A typical real estate transaction may take between

_____

_____

_____

_____

_____

9.   What items must be completed in order for the closing timeline to be met?

_____

_____

_____

_____

_____

_____

10. If the delay will be lengthy, create undue hardship for either party, or is objectionable to either party, what might occur?

_____

_____

_____

_____

_____

1. The _____ will dictate the _____ _____ and _____ that must be met so the transaction may proceed to closing.

2. A sales agreement that is correctly prepared and endorsed is a _____ _____ that holds each applicable party _____ for the _____ negotiated within the contract.

3. The format of the signature should _____ all of the other _____ _____ and _____ included within the package.

4. When a mortgage lender is involved in the transaction there may be _____ _____ or actions necessary to _____ the closing that do not exist when the transaction is set between private parties.

5. The description of the property should include

_____

_____

_____

_____

_____

_____

6. All applicable actions and documents detailed within the sales contract should be completed

_____

_____

_____

_____

_____

_____

7. Upon receipt of the sales agreement, the escrow agent should note what financial details?

_____

_____

_____

_____

_____

_____

8. Seller concessions are

_____

_____

_____

_____

_____

_____

9. If a specific inspection is dictated by the sales agreement, the settlement agent should note

_____

_____

_____

_____

_____

_____

10.   Name five specific terms relating to the title that should be noted

_____

_____

_____

_____

_____

11.   What does a real estate sales contract outline?

_____

_____

_____

_____

_____

12.   List five common alternate names you might encounter for a real estate sales contract.

_____

_____

_____

_____

_____

13.   List three alternate names commonly used for the contract for deed.

_____

_____

_____

_____

14.   Under a contract for deed, who holds legal title to the property?

_____

_____

_____

_____

_____

15.   What does the buyer gain under a contract for deed?

_____

_____

_____

_____

_____

16.   Who may assign their interest in the property under a contract for deed?

_____

_____

_____

_____

_____

17.   Explain the purpose of an option to purchase

_____

_____

_____

_____

_____

18.   What three possible avenues must you explore when you discover an option to
       purchase in the chain of title?

_____

_____

_____

_____

_____

_____

1.   Any matter that becomes a _____ , _____ or other
      matter against the property must be _____ either prior to
      close or at closing so that all parties understand what the transfer of the property
      entails.

2.   Title insurance is the guarantee of what the buyer is receiving when they _____
      _____ a piece of real property.

3.   Title insurance remains in effect until the _____ that is being
      insured is _____ .

4.   Deeds will sometimes contain _____ as to what an individual
      owner _____ or _____ do with their property.

5.   An abstract of title is
      _____
      _____
      _____
      _____
      _____
      _____

6.   The abstractor will locate specifics of the property such as _____
      _____
      _____
      _____
      _____

7.   The obtainment of insurance provides the buyer with the assurance

_____

_____

_____

_____

_____

8.   Provide three examples of why title insurance could become a critical element in the
      status of a buyer in the future

_____

_____

_____

_____

_____

9.   If a matter discovered during the title search must be cured, what affect will this have
      on the closing date?

_____

_____

_____

_____

_____

_____

10.   The title abstractor will search various locations including

_____

_____

_____

_____

_____

1. Explain the purpose of the deed

_____

_____

_____

_____

_____

2. What is considered the best deed a buyer can obtain from a seller?

_____

_____

_____

_____

_____

3. What does a grant deed warrant?

_____

_____

_____

_____

_____

4.   What does a bargain and sale deed warrant? _____

_____

_____

_____

_____

_____

5.   What is the purpose of a correction deed? _____

_____

_____

_____

_____

_____

6.   The physical transfer of a deed before the death of the grantor is known as

_____

_____

_____

_____

_____

7.   List five of the most common covenants you may find in a deed of transfer

_____

_____

_____

_____

_____

8.	Explain the purpose of an exception in a deed. _____

_____

_____

_____

_____

_____

9.	The basic bargain and sale deed contains no _____ and only the
	minimal _____ _____ of a deed.

10.	A quitclaim deed provides _____

_____

_____

_____

_____

_____

Name:
Settlement Agent Review Questions
Chapter 9 – How Title is Held and Transferred
Score:
Instructor

1. Concurrent ownership held by _____ or more _____

2. The term guardianship refers to the _____ of the property and interest of a _____ or _____ individual.

3. Any _____ taken by any _____ will affect the title to the property you are closing.

4. The types of ownership are important for you to understand so that you may:

    _____

    _____

    _____

    _____

    _____

5. Name the five unities that may exist.

    _____

    _____

    _____

    _____

    _____

6.   Name the forms of tenancy.

_____

_____

_____

_____

_____

7.   Name five special entity or individual owners whose interest in real property may require special items of scrutiny.

_____

_____

_____

_____

_____

8.   Sole ownership may be held by

_____

_____

_____

_____

9.   Tenancy by Severalty is also known as sole ownership and means that the ownership of a property is

_____

_____

_____

_____

10.   Concurrent owners share

_____

_____

_____

_____

_____

_____

1.   A promissory note is a _____ between the _____
       and the _____.

2.   If a transaction includes seller financing, the _____ is actually the
       _____

3.   The buyer will often be asked to sign a statement _____ their
       _____.

4.   The buyer will often be asked to sign a statement confirming their understanding of
       the_____ dictated through the mortgage
       and note documents.

5.   A mortgage causes the _____ to be secured against
       _____ rather than other property or as an unsecured
       personal loan.

6.   While you should gain a familiarity with the closing documents you will witness, you
       should direct any questions pertaining to the inclusions and specifics _____

       _____

       _____

       _____

       _____

       _____

7. The inclusions and specifics of the note and mortgage documents should be addressed by the _____

_____

_____

_____

_____

_____

8. What elements must a note contain to be considered binding? _____

_____

_____

_____

_____

_____

9. The buyer will be given a monthly payment breakdown at the closing that details

_____

_____

_____

_____

_____

10. The mortgage servicing transfer disclosure notice is _____

_____

_____

_____

_____

_____

Name:
Settlement Agent Review Questions
Chapter 11 – Verification and Certification
Score:
Instructor

1. If any questions pertaining to any document should arise during the settlement meeting, you should

    _____

    _____

    _____

    _____

    _____

2. If there is no company or individual available to answer any questions that arise, what actions should be taken with regard to specific questions about the transaction or documents?

    _____

    _____

    _____

    _____

    _____

3. The itemization of amount financed shows

    _____

    _____

    _____

    _____

4.   The Itemization of Amount Financed will include _____

_____

_____

_____

_____

_____

5.   The limited power of attorney granted to the settlement agent of specific mortgage
       lender provides _____

_____

_____

_____

_____

_____

6.   The limited power of attorney _____
       that the signor will receive a copy of all altered documents.

7.   The limited power of attorney specifically excludes alterations to the _____

_____

_____

_____

_____

_____

8.   A tax certificate details _____

_____

_____

_____

_____

_____

9.	If property taxes for the subject property being closed are in a delinquency status, the tax certificate will detail

_____

_____

_____

_____

_____

10.	What does it mean to escrow taxes and insurance?

_____

_____

_____

_____

_____

11.	What is the purpose of TIL?

_____

_____

_____

_____

_____

12.	When the credit report plays a role in the funds obtained, a disclosure will be provided explaining

_____

_____

_____

_____

_____

13. The signature affidavit will be a sampling of _____

_____

_____

_____

_____

_____

14. The buyer and lender will _____ the manner in which
_____ , _____ and other recurring outside
billings will be handheld.

Name:
Settlement Agent Review Questions
Chapter 12 – Pro-rata Calculations
Score:
Instructor

1. What is the purpose of prorating?

_____

_____

_____

_____

_____

2. Prorations may be based on

_____

_____

_____

_____

_____

3. Name five items commonly subject to prorating

_____

_____

_____

_____

_____

4.   What is the customary calculation base for the pro-rata calculations?

_____

_____

_____

_____

_____

5.   The four items you must determine before beginning the pro-rata calculations are

_____

_____

_____

_____

_____

6.   If taxes due have not been paid by the seller, the sellers tax portion will be

_____

_____

_____

_____

_____

7.   Special assessments for items such as street improvements and water lines

_____

_____

_____

_____

_____

8.   The entry of each prorated item will be included _____

_____

_____

_____

_____

_____

Name:
Settlement Agent Review Questions
Chapter 13 – HUD 1
Score:
Instructor

1.   What is a settlement statement?

_____

_____

_____

_____

_____

_____

2.   The settlement statement will be considered

_____

_____

_____

_____

_____

3.   The seller's portion of the settlement statement

_____

_____

_____

_____

_____

4.   Included in the seller's portion of the HUD 1 will be _____

_____

_____

_____

_____

5.   POC items are those that are _____

_____

_____

_____

_____

6.   POC fees commonly include items such as _____

_____

_____

_____

_____

7.   All financial matters _____ to the _____ will be included on the settlement   statement.

8.   All parties will _____ the settlement statement to confirm that they _____ and _____ with the inclusion.

Name:
Settlement Agent Review Questions
Chapter 14 – Signing and Post Close
Score:
Instructor

1. The closing instructions result from _____

_____

_____

_____

_____

_____

2. Closing instructions will be generated using pertinent information from the _____

_____

_____

_____

_____

_____

3. The closing instructions you will receive are _____

_____

_____

_____

_____

4. The closing instructions will specify the _____

_____

_____

_____

_____

5. The final entry on most instructions will be _____

_____

_____

_____

_____

6. What is often the last step that must be taken in order for the lender to release transaction funds? _____

_____

_____

_____

_____

7. What are the common checks that will be paid from the settlement funds? _____

_____

_____

_____

_____

8.   What is the purpose of the public recordation of the transaction documents?

_____

_____

_____

_____

_____

9.   Recording of the transaction documents at the courthouse provides what form of notice to the public?

_____

_____

_____

_____

_____

10.   What happens to the certification of recordation?

_____

_____

_____

_____

_____

11.   All parties will _____ the settlement statement to confirm that they _____ and _____ with the inclusion.

Name:
Settlement Agent Review Questions
Chapter 15 – RESPA
Score:
Instructor

1. RESPA stands for _____

_____

_____

_____

_____

_____

2. Who enforces RESPA? _____

_____

_____

_____

_____

_____

3. RESPA deals with _____

_____

_____

_____

_____

_____

4. The purposes of RESPA are to:

_____

_____

_____

_____

_____

5. RESPA prohibits

_____

_____

_____

_____

_____

6. RESPA restricts

_____

_____

_____

_____

_____

7. What limitations are placed with regard to property tax and insurance payments?

_____

_____

_____

_____

_____

Section

3

Self-Test Answer Keys

Introduction

1. Transfer or purchase transaction is completed

2. Closing Escrow
   Holding a Settlement Meeting

3. Gift Funds Seller Concessions   Loan Funding Any other source available to the borrower

4. Review each document for accuracy and completeness

   Provide the documents to each party for signature

   Provide basic explanations for the documents

   Witness the signing of the documents

5. The division of ongoing expenses or income items between the buyer and the seller
   Primary Lenders with excess deposits

Chapter 1 – Types of Meetings

1. confirm signatures

   witness signatures

2. reviewed

   stipulations

3. act

   signature

   confirmation

   transfer

4. representative

5. not escrow

6. Round Table Meeting / Escrow

7. All parties pertinent to the transaction will sit down simultaneously to complete their legal

8. A set of closing instructions specific to their needs in the transaction

9. Every task has been completed or a waiver nullifying the need for a specifically negotiated items has been received from the applicable parties

10. Legal authorization that enables them to act on behalf of a missing party

11. Pertinent to the transaction will sit down simultaneously to complete their legal requirements

Chapter 2 – Party Obligations

1. real estate purchase agreement

   guide

2. four

3. The executable deed including any covenants and warranties agreed upon by the parties

   The most recent property tax bill for the property being transferred

   An insurance policy showing current coverage on the property if such a requirement has been negotiated in the sales agreement

   The termite or other inspection as negotiated within the sales agreement

   Deeds or documents showing the removal of any liens or encumbrances discovered during the title search or required by the negotiated sales agreement or lender commitment

   A title commitment and insurance policy

   A survey or survey affidavit

An offset statement or statement by an owner or lien holder as to the exact balance due on a lien held against the property

Keys to the property

If the property is an income producing property, any documents securing or confirming this income

4. Funds available for the purchase price negotiated for the property, settlement costs and any matters that the buyer has agreed to pay before settlement

5. Specific documents for the buyer to sign at the settlement meeting

6. Mortgage   Note   Riders   Addendums

   Any other document they deem necessary to solidify the repayment requirement of the funds provided for the transaction

7. Determine if a valid contract exists, that illustrates the negotiations of the transaction

   Confirm that all parties to the transaction are legally authorized to conduct legal actions through competency, resident status and legal age verification

   Verify that each party is being fairly compensated for the exchange being made through the transaction

   Determine that a legal parcel or property is being transferred between the properties

   Confirm that all parties to the transactions are legally authorized to conduct legal actions through competency, resident status and legal age verification.

8. A statement by an owner or lien holder as to the exact balance due on a lien held against the property

9. That they understand the items they are to bring with them to closing

10. Oversee settlement meeting

    Confirm the identity and legal authority of all parties at the meeting

    Oversee the signing of all documents

    Close escrow

Record applicable documents

Pay off all matters

Chapter 3 – Meeting Overviews

1. appointed / act

2. record / legal names

3. neutral / buyer / seller

4. legal form / identification

5. details / document / actions / closing instructions

6. current loan balance / documents / loan assumption

7. a closing statement / HUD-1

8. will not be present at the time of the closing

9. these funds will be transferred to the settlement agent and become available for disbursement upon confirmation by the lender that all loan conditions have been satisfied

10. every action that each party must complete before the deed is delivered to the buyer and the purchase funds are delivered to the seller

Chapter 4 – Opening Escrow

1. fees / affinity service providers

2. offset statement / cleared

3. expected close date / sales contract

4. Review the information included in the order and confirm that all of the data that will be needed to proceed is included within the ordering documents

5. date of order

Property address

The names and addresses of all owners who hold interest in the property

The sales price agreed upon for the purchase of the property

The amount (if any) of the earnest money paid

The allocation of the earnest money

The amount, if any, of additional funds placed in escrow or other locations to be credited toward the transaction

6. seller finance / seller concessions / lender funds

   any conditions relating to these financial matters

7. name of the real estate agent

   the commission payment that the real estate agent will receive in the transaction

8. Property Description

   Sale inclusions or exclusions any inspections or reports that must be satisfactorily received

9. the buyer / the seller / the real estate agent / the lender

   another party pertinent to your transaction

10. the exact names of the individuals who will be taking title to the property

Chapter 5 – Potential Delays

1. closing date / sales contract

2. addendum / sales agreement / extends

3. service bills / billings / party

4. last / completion

5. the date the buyer wishes to take possession of the property

   The date the seller wishes to relinquish possession of the property

   The date the seller requires the purchase funds paid for the property

6. the completion of the loan application

   Documentation process to obtain the required purchase money

   The date the seller requires the purchase funds for another purchase

7. the completion of a title search on the subject property

   The issuance of a title insurance policy

   The completion of an appraisal

   The completion of a termite or other inspection report as desired by the buyer, seller, or mortgage lender

8. 15 and 60 days to complete

9. property and owner searches / inspections / loan stipulations / other matters as negotiated in the sales contract

10. a release will be signed by both the buyer and the seller relieving all parties from their obligations under the contract

Chapter 6 – The Sales Contract

1. sales contract / obligations / agreements

2. binding contract / responsible / terms

3. match / documents / instructions

4. additional requirements / fund

5. physical address / city name / county name / deed information

6. on or before the expected closing date set in the transaction

7. the division of transaction expense outlined within the sales contract

   The date set for the pro-rata of fixed expense

   The inclusion or exclusion of mortgage funds and contingency clauses

   The allocation of seller concessions toward closing

   The amount of any earnest money deposits received in relationship to the transaction

8. the specific amount of funds a seller will allocate toward paying a buyer's closing costs out of a sellers closing proceeds

9. information detailing who will pay for the inspection

   When payment for the inspection will be made

   Details pertaining to the actions that will ensue if an inspection is not satisfactory

10. the marketability of the title

   the ability to insure the title

   restrictions specific to the property

   Easements, rights and privileges costs pertaining to the search survey completion and costs

11. all the terms and conditions of the sale between a buyer and a seller

12. offer to purchase

   option to buy or sell

   sales agreement

   contract for deed

   contract for purchase

13 land contract

article of agreement

installment land contract

14. the seller

15. possession of the property and equitable title

16. both parties may assign their interest in the property

17. an option to purchase real property is a contract that allows the right to purchase the property to a specific individual at a specific price and within a specific time period

18. establish that the option conveyed has expired in time

Establish that an additional document was created terminating the option

Chapter 7 – The Title Search

1. defect / restriction / addressed

2. purchase

3. interest transferred

4. restrictions / may / may not

5. the summary of all recorded documents filed within the public records system that apply to a particular parcel of land

6. the exact description

The estate or interest held by the seller of the property

Any exceptions such as liens, encumbrances, or other defects that exist in relationship to the subject property

Any items or actions take against the property owner that might affect the title to the property

Any other matter that appears in public record with applicability to the transaction may require additional research and become part of the title commitment, exceptions or insurance issuances

7. that if any item was missed during the search process, the buyer will not be responsible for any costs that might arise in the future in relationship to a lack of knowledge

8. a deed could contain a clerical error

    Incorrect marital rights might have been entered on a deed of conveyance

    Undisclosed heirs in a past property transfer might come forth to claim interest in the property

    The signature on a deed transfer documentation by any individual deemed unable to sign such documents like a minor or an incompetent individual

9. additional delays in the closing process may occur while the matter is addressed

10. the county recorders office / the county assessor's office / other taxing agency records / any pendens indexes / other public records specific to the property or seller

Chapter 8 - Deeds

1. A deed conveys or transfers ownership interest in land from one person to another

2. general warranty deed

3. the seller who provides a grant-deed warrants only the time that particular owner had possession of the title

4. the bargain and sale deed contains no warranties or covenants.

5. a correction deed is used to correct an error in a previously executed document

6. actual delivery

7. Covenant of seizin

    Covenant of enjoyment

Covenant against encumbrances

Covenant of further assurance

Covenant of right to convey

Covenant of Non-Claim

8. an exception is included to withhold or exclude part of the estate or land being conveyed from the transfer

9. covenants / essentials

10. contains no warranties / contains no covenants

   does not promise the seller even holds interest in the property

Chapter 9 – How Title is Held and Transferred

1. two / individuals

2. administration / minor / incompetent

3. action / interested owner

4. Ensure that you have a full understanding of all potential owners who may have obtained an interest to a piece of real property so that you may ensure that any outstanding interests are removed prior to the close of escrow

5. Unity of Time

   Unity of Title

   Unity of Possession

   Unity of Interest

   Unity of Person

6. Tenancy by the Entirety / Joint Tenancy / Tenancy in Common

7. Business Trusts

   Credit Unions

   Corporations

   Aliens

   Convicts

   Government Entities

   Banks or Savings Institutions

8. An Individual

   Married Couples

   Corporations designed as a single entity

9. Cut off from other individuals and the named individual owns the property alone

10. The Property / Unity / Ownership Interest

Chapter 10 – Loan Commitment and Security Instruments

1. contract / borrower / lender

2. lender / seller

3. confirming / mailing address

4. monthly payment

5. note / real property

6. to the individual or company that generated the documents

7. mortgage lender / loan processor / closing team at the lending institution

8. the note must be in writing

The note must be between a borrower and a lender, both of whom have the ability to enter into a legally binding contract

The note will state the borrowers promise to pay a certain sum of money and the terms under which those monies will be paid

9. PMI / School Taxes / County Taxes / Insurance Premiums

   Any services required under the mortgage agreement

10. Define any mortgage servicing information known to the mortgage lender at the time of closing and the record of historical transfers of servicing activity by the lender

Chapter 11 – Verification and Certification

1. Direct the question to the company or individual who created the applicable signature requirement

2. the services of a competent attorney should be obtained to gain the needed clarification

3. a legal disclosure document from the lender to the borrower of funds

4. items paid by the lender on the borrower's behalf and then financed as part of the transaction

5. for these specific individuals to correct the typographical or clerical errors on behalf of the signor

6. expressly states

7. interest rate

   term

   principal balance

   principal and interest payments

   index or margin of an adjustable rate loan

8. the applicable tax records for the subject property being closed to determine the current payment status

9. the exact payment amount

    the date that the tax billing became delinquent

    the taxing authority to which the applicable taxes are owed

10. the buyer will pay a portion of these bills to the lender with each monthly payment

    The lender will then hold the portional payments in an escrow account until the billings become due

    The lender then makes payments for these billings

11. to disclose to the borrower the true cost of the credit that they are obtaining

12. The scores received from the bureaus

    The factors contributing to the scores

    The fact that the bureaus do not make a credit determination but rather report the inclusions of the credit profile

13. possible signatures of the buyer

14. negotiate / taxes / insurance

Chapter 12 – Pro-Rata Calculations

1. to allow the buyer and seller to split the cost and income fairly according to the term of ownership

2. the date of closing another term as negotiated within the sales contract

3. real estate taxes

    homeowner's insurance premiums

    rents received on income producing property

    Other income received from property

expenses incurred on an income producing property

Oil or other fuel tank filling costs

any utility billing not turned off and paid in full prior to closing

Any other negotiated matter

4. A 30 day month

5. the number of times taxes are assessed per year the due date of each tax billing cycle

   the status of the payment of the taxes

   the period of time each payment covers

6. deducted from the funds received by the seller at the closing table

7. are typically not prorated

8. in the final settlement statement

Chapter 13– HUD 1

1. HUD 1 that is a statement that itemizes all closing costs payable at the closing or settlement meeting

2. the final authority of all transaction calculations and as such, is a very important document at the closing table

3. breaks down all items on the seller's behalf

4. any liens or mortgages that must be paid to secure a clear title to the property

   Any seller concession toward the buyers closing costs (as negotiated in the sales agreement)

   Any additional charges for which the seller is responsible

   Any prorated items the seller has agreed to pay as negotiated in the sales agreements

Any other costs the seller has incurred that must be paid at the closing table

5. paid outside of closing before settlement

6. credit reports / appraisals / inspections

   other matters that the borrower ordered

7. pertinent / transaction agent

8. sign / understand / agree

Chapter 14 – Signing and Post Close

1. the specifics of all of the tasks and processes that led to the closing

2. sales agreement / addendums / contingencies / title report / financing conditions

   Any other matter that occurred during the preparatory phase of the real estate transfer

3. a detailing of the exact steps you must take to finalize the closing

4. various conditions and tasks that must be completed at the actual settlement to legally transfer ownership of the subject property

5. the authorization to disperse funds to the parties owed money in the transaction

6. the providing of the fully endorsed documents to the mortgage lender for review

7. mortgage loans or liens for which the seller is responsible

   The sellers portion of the purchase proceeds

   Any billings that are linked to the transaction such as appraisal fees or inspection costs

   Any commission due to the real estate agents

   Any other matter that is listed on the instructions or for which an agreed upon bill has been presented during the period leading to the closing

8. to provide security to the buyer, lender, and seller because it makes public all records of the transaction

9. constructive notice

10. this document will become a part of the transaction file and will enable anyone who reviews the file to see who completed the recording functions

Chapter 15 - RESPA

1. Real Estate Settlement Procedures Act

2. HUD

3. closing cost and settlement procedures

4. regulate the processes of closing practices in the United States

   Help consumers in shopping for settlement services

   Eliminate referral fees that increase the costs of certain settlement services

5. specific practices in relationship to the transfer of property that involves a first mortgage loan on a one to four unit dwelling

   A person from giving or accepting any thing of value for referrals of settlement services or businesses

   A person from giving or accepting any part of the charge for services that are not performed

6. the amount of property tax and insurance payments that may be paid in advance at or prior to the closing

7. the amount of property tax and insurance payments that may be paid by a borrower in advance is limited to the owner's share of the taxes and insurance that is due at the time of settlement plus $1/6^{th}$ of the amount that will become due for these items within a 12-month period

Closing Review Forms

NOTICE: The enclosed forms are for example purposes only. The applicable forms have been generated using the publicly released and acceptable versions as released by the applicable agency. Neither the publisher nor the author warrants the use of these forms. The individual making use of the applicable form accepts all responsibility for the use and for confirming the completeness, contents or applicability of said forms. The inclusion of these forms is not to be considered legal advice. The reader is encouraged to seek the advice of a real estate attorney or other professional prior to using the enclosed forms.

TIMETABLE	
Week 1	Receive Escrow Order
	Review Sales Contract
Week 1 – 2	Order Preliminary Title Report
	Open Escrow Account
	Order Pest Inspections
	Comply with Sale Agreement Terms / Orders
Week 3	Receive Lender Instructions
	Review Preliminary Title Report
	Review Inspections
	Order Pay Off Summary or Defect Cure Actions Indicated by the Title Report
Week 3-4	Prepare Escrow Instructions
	Complete Pro-Rata Calculations
	Generate Settlement Statement
	Prepare Loan Documents
Week 4	Hold Settlement Meeting
	Sign Documents
	Close Escrow
	Record Documents
	Release Funds
	Pay off all matters

ESCROW PROPERTY:

Date: _____ Ordering Individual: _____

Subject Property: _____

Owner: _____ Co-Owner: _____

Address: _____

Telephone Number: _____ Alternate Number: _____

Buyer: _____ Co-Buyer: _____

Current Address: _____

Telephone Number: _____ Alternate Number: _____

TRANSACTION DETAILS

Sales Price: $_____ Earnest Money Paid: _____

Total Down Payment (Including Deposit: $_____

Other Finance Specifics: _____

_____

Seller Agent Commission: $_____ ___% Paid to: _____

Buyer Agent Commission: $_____ ___% Paid to: _____

1st Mortgage Lender: _____ Amount: _____

Terms: _____

Other liens to be paid: _____ Amount: _____

Terms: _____

Inspections and Reports: _____

_____

Closing Date: _____ Closing Costs: _____

Special Closing Notes: _____

_____

Names to appear on title: _____

Other Notes: _____

STANDARD AGREEMENT FOR THE SALE OF REAL ESTATE

<table>
<tr><td colspan="2">SELLERS BUISNES RELATIONSHIP WITH LICENSED BROKER</td></tr>
<tr><td>Broker (company) _____</td><td>Phone _____</td></tr>
<tr><td>Address _____</td><td>Fax _____</td></tr>
<tr><td>Licensee(s) _____</td><td>Designated Agent __ Yes __ No</td></tr>
<tr><td colspan="2">BROKER IS THE AGENT FOR THE SELLER   OR (if checked below):</td></tr>
<tr><td colspan="2">Broker is NOT the Agent for the seller and is a/an: __ AGENT FOR BUYER __ Transaction Licensee</td></tr>
</table>

<table>
<tr><td colspan="2" align="center">BUYERS BUISNES RELATIONSHIP WITH LICENSED BROKER</td></tr>
<tr><td>Broker (company) _____</td><td>Phone _____</td></tr>
<tr><td>Address _____</td><td>Fax _____</td></tr>
<tr><td>Licensee(s) _____</td><td>Designated Agent __ Yes __ No</td></tr>
<tr><td colspan="2">BROKER IS THE AGENT FOR THE BUYER   OR (if checked below):</td></tr>
<tr><td colspan="2">Broker is NOT the Agent for the seller and is a/an: __ AGENT FOR SELLER __ Transaction Licensee</td></tr>
</table>

When the same Broker is Agent for Buyer, Broker is a Dual Agent. All of Broker's licensees are also Dual Agents UNLESS there is a separate Designated Agents for Buyer and Seller. If the same Licensee is designated for Seller and Buyer, the Licensee is a Dual Agent.

1. *This Agreement*, dated _____ is between
   SELLER(S): _____, called Seller, and
   BUYER(S): _____ , called Buyer.
2. PROPERTY Seller herby agrees to sell and convey to Buyer, who hereby agrees to purchase:
   ALL THAT CERTAIN lot or piece of ground with buildings and improvements thereon erected, if any, known as:

   _____
   _____

   In the _____ of _____ County of _____ in the State of
   _____. Identification (e.g., Tax ID#, Parcel #; Lot, Block; Deed Book, Page,
   Recording Date): _____

3. TERMS
   (A) Purchase Price _____
   U.S. Dollars which will be paid to the Seller by the Buyer as follows:
   1. Cash or check at the signing of this Agreement_____ $ _____
   2. Cash or check within _____ days of the execution of this agreement_____ $ _____
   3. _____ $ _____
   4. Cash or cashiers check at the time of settlement_____ $ _____
                                                TOTAL $ _____

   (B) Deposits paid by Buyer within _____ DAYS of settlement will be by cash or cashiers check. Deposits, regardless of the form of payment and the person designated as payee, will be paid in U.S. Dollars to Broker for Seller (unless otherwise stated here) _____
   _____ who will retain deposits in an escrow account until consummation or termination of this Agreement in conformity with all applicable laws and regulations. Any check tendered as deposit monies may be held uncashed pending the acceptance of this agreement.
   (C) Seller's written approval to be on or before _____
   (D) Settlement to be on _____ or before if Buyer and Seller agree
   (E) Settlement will occur in the county where the Property is located or in an adjacent county, during normal business hours, unless Buyer and Seller agree otherwise.
   (F) Conveyance from Seller will be by fee simple deed of Special Warranty unless otherwise stated here
   _____
   (G) Payment of transfer taxes will be divided equally between Buyer and Seller unless otherwise stated here
   _____
   (H) At the time of settlement, the following will be adjusted pro-rata on a daily basis between Buyer and Seller, reimbursing where applicable current taxes (see Information regarding Real Estate Taxes), rents, interest on mortgage assumptions, condominium fees, and home owners association fees, water and or sewer fees together with any other lienable municipal services.

Figure 6:1 Sample Sales Contract Page 1

4. **FIXTURES & PERSONAL PROPERTY**
   (A) INCLUDED in this sale are all existing items, permanently installed in the Property, free of liens, including plumbing, heating, lighting fixtures (including chandeliers and ceiling fans); water treatment systems; pool and spa equipment; garage door openers and transmitters; television antennas; unspotted shrubbery, plantings and trees; any remaining heating and cooking fuels stored on the Property at the time of settlement; sump pumps; storage sheds; mailboxes; wall to wall carpeting; existing window screens, storm windows and screen storm doors, window covering hardware, shades and blinds; awnings; built-in air conditioners, built in appliances; and the range unless otherwise stated. Also
   included:_____
   (B) LEASED items (not owned by Seller): _____
   (C) EXCLUDED fixtures and items: _____

5. **DATES / TIME IS OF THE ESSENCE**
   (A) The settlement date and all other dates and times referred to for the performance of the obligations of this Agreement are of the essence and are binding.
   (B) For purposes of this Agreement, the number of days will be counted from the date of execution, excluding the day this Agreement was executed and including the last day of the time period. The Execution Date of this Agreement is the date when Buyer and Seller have indicated full acceptance of this Agreement by signing and/or initialing it. All changes to this Agreement should be initialed and dated.
   (C) The settlement date is not extended by any other provision of this Agreement and may only be extended by mutual written Agreement of the parties.
   (D) Certain time periods are pre-printed in this Agreement as a convenience to the Buyer and Seller. All pre-printed time periods are negotiable and may be changed by striking out the pre-printed text and inserting a different time period acceptable to all parties.

6. **MORTGAGE CONTINGENCY**
   ___ WAIVED This sales is NOT contingent on mortgage financing, although Buyer may still obtain mortgage financing.
   ___ ELECTED
   (A) The sale is contingent on Buyer obtaining mortgage financing as follows:

First Mortgage on the Property	Second Mortgage on the Property
Loan Amount $_____	Loan Amount $_____
Minimum Term _____ years	Minimum Term _____ years
Type of Mortgage _____	Type of Mortgage _____
Mortgage Lender _____	Mortgage Lender _____
_____	_____
Interest Rate _____% however, Buyer agrees to accept the interest rate as may be committed by the mortgage lender, not to exceed a maximum interest rate of _____%. Discount points, loan origination, loan placement, and other fees charged by the lender as a percentage of the mortgage loan (excluding any mortgage insurance premiums or VA funding fee) not to exceed _____% (1% if not specified)	Interest Rate _____% however, Buyer agrees to accept the interest rate as may be committed by the mortgage lender, not to exceed a maximum interest rate of _____%. Discount points, loan origination, loan placement, and other fees charged by the lender as a percentage of the mortgage loan (excluding any mortgage insurance premiums or VA funding fee) not to exceed _____% (1% if not specified)

   The interest rate(s) and fee(s) provisions in paragraph 6(A) are satisfied if the mortgage lender(s) gives Buyer the right to guarantee the interest rate(s) and fee(s) at or before the maximum levels stated. Buyer gives Seller the right at Seller's sole option and as permitted by law and the mortgage lender(s) to contribute financially, without promise of reimbursement to the buyer and or the mortgage lender(s) to make the above mortgage terms available to the Buyer.
   (B) Within _____ days (10 if not specified) from the Execution Date of this Agreement, Buyer will make a completed, written mortgage application for the mortgage terms stated above to the mortgage lender(s) defined in paragraph 6(A), if any, otherwise to a responsible mortgage lender(s) of Buyer's choice. Broker for Buyer, if any, otherwise Broker for Seller, is authorized to communicate with the mortgage lender(s) to assist in the mortgage loan process.
   (C) Should Buyer furnish false or incomplete information to Seller, Broker(s), or the mortgage lender(s) concerning Buyer's legal or financial status, or fail to cooperate in good faith in processing the mortgage loan application, which results in the mortgage lender(s) refusing to approve a mortgage loan commitment, Buyer will be in default of this Agreement.
   (D) 1. Mortgage commitment date: _____ if Seller does not receive a copy of Buyer's mortgage commitment by this date, Buyer and Seller agree to extend the mortgage commitment date until the Seller terminated this Agreement buy written notice to the Buyer
   2. Upon receiving a mortgage commitment, Buyer will promptly deliver a copy of the commitment to the Seller.
   3. Seller may terminate this Agreement, in writing, after the mortgage commitment date, if the mortgage commitment
      a. is not valid until the date of settlement , OR
      b. is conditional upon the sale and settlement of any other property, OR
      c. does not satisfy all the mortgage terms as stated in paragraph 6(A), OR
      d. Contains any other conditions not specified in this Agreement that is not satisfied and or removed in writing by the mortgage lender(s)

Figure 6:2 Sample Sales Contract

4. If this Agreement is terminated pursuant to paragraph 6(D)(1) or (3), or the mortgage loan(s) is not obtained for settlement, all deposit monies will be returned to Buyer according to the terms of paragraph 30 and this Agreement will be VOID. Buyer will be responsible for any costs incurred by Buyer for any inspections or certifications obtained according to the terms of this Agreement and any costs incurred by Buyer for (1) Title search, title insurance and or mechanics' lien insurance, or any fee for cancellation. (2) Flood insurance and or fire insurance with extended coverage, mine subsidence insurance or any fee for cancellation (3) Appraisal fee and charges paid in advance to mortgage lender(s)

(E) If the mortgage lender(s), or an insurer providing property and casualty insurance s required by the mortgage lender(s), requires repairs to the Property, Buyer will, upon receiving the requirements, deliver a copy of the requirements to the Seller. Within ___ DAYS of receiving the copy of the requirements, Seller will notify Buyer whether Seller will make the required repairs at Seller's expense.

    1. If Seller makes the required repairs to the satisfaction of the mortgage lender(s) or insurer, Buyer accepts the Property and agrees to the RELEASE in paragraph 27 of this Agreement.

    2. If Seller will not make the required repairs, or if Seller fails to respond within the time given, Buyer will, within ___ days, notify Seller of Buyer's choice to:

        a. Make the required repairs, at Buyer's expense, with permission and access to the Property given by Seller; permission and access may not be unreasonably withheld by Seller, OR

        b. Terminate this Agreement by written notice to Seller, with all deposit monies returned to Buyer according to the terms of paragraph 30 of this Agreement.

(F) **Seller Assist**

    __ NOT APPLICABLE

    __ APPLICABLE, Seller will pay:

        $_____, or _____% of Purchase Price, maximum, toward Buyer's costs as acceptable to the mortgage lender(s)

<hr>

FHA/VA, IF APPLIABLE

(G) It is expressly agreed that notwithstanding any other provisions of this contract, Buyer will not be obligated to complete the purchase of the Property described herein or to incur any penalty by forfeiture of earnest money deposits or otherwise unless Buyer has been given, in accordance with HUD/FHA or VA requirements, a written statement by the Federal Housing Commissioner, Veterans Administration, or a Direct Endorsement Lender setting forth the appraised value of the Property of not less than $_____ (the dollar amount to be inserted is the sales price as stated in this Agreement). Buyer will have the privilege and option of proceeding with consummation of the contract without regard to the amount of the appraised valuation. The appraised valuation is arrived at to determine the maximum mortgage the Department of Housing and Urban Development will insure. HUD does not warrant the value nor the condition of the Property as acceptable.

Warning: Section 1010 of Title 18, U.S.C., Department of Housing and Urban Development and Federal Housing Administration Transactions, provides, "Whoever for the purpose of... influencing in any way the action of such Department, makes, passes, utters or publishes any statement, knowing the same to be false... shall be fined under this title or imprisoned not more than two years or both."

(H) **U.S. Department of Housing and Urban Development (HUD) NOTICE TO PURCHASERS: Buyer's Acknowledgement**

    __ Buyer has received the HUD Notice "For Your Protection: Get a Home Inspection." Buyer understands the importance of getting an independent home inspection and has thought about this before signing this Agreement. Buyer understands that FHA will not perform a home inspection nor guarantee the price or condition of the Property.

(I) **Certification** We the undersigned, Seller(s) and Buyer(s) party to this transaction each certify that the terms of this contract for purchase are true to the best of our knowledge and believe, and that any other agreement entered into by any of these parties in connection with this transaction is attached to this Agreement.

7. **WAIVER OF CONTINGENCIES**

If this Agreement is contingent on Buyer's right to inspect and/or repair the Property, or to verify insurability, environmental conditions, boundaries, certifications, zoning classification or use, or any other information regarding the Property, Buyer's failure to exercise any of Buyer's options within the times set forth in this Agreement is a WAIVER of that contingency and Buyer accepts the Property and agrees to the RELEASE in paragraph 27 of this Agreement.

8. **PROPERTY INSURANCE AVAILABILITY**

    __ WAIVED. This Agreement is NOT contingent upon Buyer obtaining property and casualty insurance for the Property, although Buyer may still obtain property and casualty insurance.

    __ ELECTED. Contingency Period: ___ DAYS (15 if not specified) from the Execution Date of this Agreement.

    Within the Contingency Period, Buyer will make application for property and casualty insurance for the Property to a responsible insurer. **Broker for Buyer, if any, otherwise Broker for Seller, may communicate with the insurer to assist in the insurance process.** If Buyer cannot obtain property and casualty insurance for the Property on terms and conditions reasonably acceptable to Buyer, Buyer will, within the Contingency Period:

    (A) Accept the Property and agree to the RELEASE in paragraph 27 of this Agreement, OR

    (B) Terminate this Agreement by written notice to Seller, with all deposit monies returned to Buyer according to the terms of paragraph 30 of this Agreement, OR

    (C) Enter into a mutually acceptable written agreement with Seller.

Figure 6:14 Sample Sales Contract

If Buyer and Seller do not reach a written agreement during the Contingency Period, and Buyer does not terminate this Agreement by written notice to Seller within that time, Buyer will accept the Property and agree to the RELEASE in paragraph 27 of this Agreement.

9. **INSPECTIONS**

   (A) Seller will provide access to insurers' representatives and, as may be required by this Agreement, to surveyors, municipal officials, and inspectors. If Buyer is obtaining mortgage financing, Seller will provide access to the Property to appraisers and others reasonably required by the mortgage lender(s). Buyer may attend any inspections.

10. INSPECTION CONTINGENCY OPTIONS

   The inspection contingencies elected by Buyer in paragraphs 11-15 are controlled by the Options set forth below. The time periods in these Options will apply to all inspection contingencies in paragraphs 11-15 unless otherwise stated in this Agreement.

   Option 1. Within the Contingency Period, as stated in paragraphs 11-15, Buyer will:

   1. Accept the Property with the information stated in the report(s) and agree to the RELEASE in paragraph 27 of this Agreement, OR
   2. If Buyer is not satisfied with the information stated in the report(s), terminate this Agreement by written notice to the Seller, with all deposit monies returned to the Buyer according to the terms of paragraph 30 of this Agreement, OR
   3. Enter into a mutually acceptable written agreement with the Seller providing for any repairs or improvements to the Property and or any credit to Buyer at settlement, as acceptable to the mortgage lender(s), if any.

   If Buyer and Seller do not reach a written agreement during the specified Contingency Period, and Buyer does not terminate this Agreement by written notice to Seller within that time, Buyer will accept the Property and agree to the RELEASE in paragraph 27 of this Agreement.

   Option 2. Within the Contingency Period, as stated in paragraphs 11-15, Buyer will:

   1. Accept the Property with the information stated in the report(s) and agree to the RELEASE in paragraph 27 of this Agreement, OR
   2. If Buyer is not satisfied with the information stated in the report(s), present the report(s) to Seller with a Written Corrective Proposal ("Proposal") listing corrections and/or credits desired by Buyer. The Proposal may, but is not required to, include the name of a properly licensed or qualified professional to perform the corrections requested in the Proposal, provisions for payment, including retests, and a projected date for completion of the corrections. Buyer agrees that Seller will not be held liable for corrections that do not comply with mortgage lender or governmental requirements if performed in a workmanlike manner according to the terms of Buyer's Proposal, or by a contractor selected by Buyer.

      a. Within ___ days (7 if not specified) of receiving Buyer's Proposal, Seller will inform Buyer in writing of Seller's choice to:
         1. Satisfy the terms of Buyer's Proposal, OR
         2. Credit Buyer at settlement for the cost to satisfy the terms of Buyer's Proposal, as acceptable to mortgage lender(s), if any, OR
         3. Not satisfy the terms of Buyer's Proposal or to credit Buyer at settlement for the costs to satisfy the terms of Buyer's Proposal.
      b. If Seller agrees to satisfy the terms of Buyer's Proposal or to credit Buyer at settlement as specified above, Buyer accepts Property and agrees to the RELEASE in paragraph 27 of this Agreement.
      c. If seller chooses not to satisfy the terms of Buyer's Proposal and not to credit Buyer at settlement as specified above, of if Seller fails to choose any option within the time give, Buyer will within ___ days (5 if not specified);
         1. Accept the Property with the information stated in the report(s) and agree to the RELEASE in paragraph 27 of this Agreement, OR
         2. Terminate this Agreement by written notice to Seller, with all deposit monies returned to Buyer according to the terms of paragraph 30 of this Agreement, OR
         3. Enter into a mutually acceptable written agreement with Seller providing for any repairs or improvements to the Property and/or any credit to Buyer at settlement, as acceptable to the mortgage lender(s) if any.

11. **PROPERTY INSPECTION CONTINGENCY** (See Property and Environmental Inspection Notices)

   Buyer understands that property inspections, certifications and/or investigations can be performed by professional contractors, home inspectors, engineers, architects and other properly licensed or otherwise qualified professionals, and may include, but are not limited to: structural components; roof; exterior windows and exterior doors; exterior siding, fascia, gutters and downspouts; swimming pools, hot tubs and spas; appliances; electrical, plumbing, heating and cooling systems; water penetration; environmental hazards (e.g., mold, fungi, indoor air quality, asbestos, underground storage tanks, etc.); electromagnetic fields; wetlands inspection; flood plain verification; property boundary/square footage verification; and any other items Buyer may select. Buyer is advised to investigate easements, deed and use restrictions (including any historic preservation restrictions or ordinances) that apply to the Property and to review local zoning ordinances. Other provisions of this Agreement may provide for inspections, certifications and/or investigations that are not waived or altered by Buyer's election here.

   ___ WAIVED Buyer has the option to conduct property inspections, certifications, and/or investigations. Buyer WAIVES THIS OPTION and agrees to the RELEASE in paragraph 27 of this agreement.

   ___ ELECTED Contingency Period: ___ days (15 if not specified) from the Execution Date of this Agreement.

   (A) Within the Contingency Period, Buyer, at Buyer's expense, may have inspections, certifications and/or investigations completed by properly licensed or otherwise qualified professionals. If Buyer elects to have a home inspection of the Property, as defined in the Pennsylvania Home Inspection Law (see Information Regarding the Home Inspection Law), the home inspection must be performed by a full member of a national home inspection association, in accordance with the ethical standards and code of conduct or practice of that association, or by a properly licensed or registered professional engineer, or a properly licensed or registered architect. This contingency does not apply to the following conditions or items:

   _____

   (B) If Buyer is not satisfied with the condition of the Property as stated in the written inspection report(s), Buyer will proceed under one of the following Options as listed in paragraph 10 within the Contingency Period:

Figure 6:17 Sample Sales Contract

    __   Option 1

    __   Option 2   For the purposes of Paragraph 11 only, Buyer agrees to accept the Property with the results of any report(s) and agrees to the RELEASE in paragraph 27 of this Agreement if the total cost to correct the conditions stated in the report(s) is less than $_____ ($0 if not specified) (the "Deductible Amount"). Otherwise, all provisions of paragraph 10, Option 2, shall apply, except that Seller will be deemed to have satisfied the terms of Buyer's Proposal if Seller agrees to perform corrections or offer credits such that the cumulative cost of any uncorrected or uncredited condition(s) is equal to the Deductible Amount.

2. WOOD INFESTATION INSPECTION CONTINGENCY

    __   WAIVED. Buyer has the option to have the Property inspected for wood infestation by an inspector certified as a wood-destroying pest pesticide applicator. BUYER WAIVES THIS OPTOIN and agrees to the RELEASE in paragraph 27 of this Agreement.

    __   ELECTED. Contingency Period ___ days (15 if not specified) from the Execution Date of this Agreement.

    (A) Within the Contingency Period, Buyer, at Buyer's expense, may obtain a written "Wood Destroying Insect Infestation Inspection Report" from an inspector certified as a wood-destroying pests pesticide applicator and will deliver it an all supporting documents and drawings provided by the inspector to Seller. The report is to be made satisfactory to and in compliance with applicable laws, mortgage lender requirements, and/or Federal Insuring and Guaranteeing Agency requirements, if any. The inspection is to be limited to all readily visible and accessible areas of all structures on the Property except fences and the following structures, which will not be inspected: _____

    (B) If the inspection reveals active infestation(s), Buyer, at Buyer's expense, may within the Contingency Period, obtain a proposal from a wood-destroying pest pesticide applicator to treat the Property.

    (C) If the inspection reveals damage from active or previous infestation(s), Buyer, at Buyer's expense, may within the Contingency Period, obtain a written report from a professional contractor, home inspector, or structural engineer that is limited to structural damage to the Property caused by wood-destroying organisms and a Proposal to repair and/or treat the Property.

    (D) If Buyer is not satisfied with the condition of the Property as stated in the written inspection report(s), Buyer will proceed under one of the following Options as listed in paragraph 10 within the Contingency Period:

        __ Option 1

        __ Option 2

3. STATUS OF RADON

    (A) Seller has no knowledge concerning the presence or absence of radon unless checked below:

        __ 1.   Seller has knowledge that the Property was tested on the dates, by the methods (e.g., charcoal canister, alpha track, etc.), and with the results of the test indicated below:

            DATE   TYPE OF TEST   RESULTS (picocuries/liter or working levels)

            _____

        __ 2.   Seller has knowledge that the Property underwent radon reduction measures on the date(s) and by the method(s) indicated below:

            DATE   RADON REDUCTION METHOD

            _____

            COPIES OF ALL AVAILABLE TEST REPORTS will be delivered to Buyer with this Agreement. SELLER DOES NOT WARRANT EITHER THE METHODS OR RESULTS OF THE TESTS.

    (B) RADON INSPECTION CONTINGENCY

        __   WAIVED. Buyer has the option to have the Property inspected for radon by a certified inspector. BUYER WAIVES THIS OPTION and agrees to the RELEASE in paragraph 27 of this Agreement.

        __   ELECTED. Contingency Period: ____ Days (15 if not specified) from the Execution Date of this Agreement.

        Within the Contingency Period, Buyer, at Buyer's expense, may obtain a radon test a radon test of the Property from a certified inspector. If Seller performs any radon remediation, Seller will provide Buyer a certification that the remediation was performed by a properly licensed and certified radon mitigation company.

        1.   If the written test report reveals the presence of radon below 0.02 working levels or 4 picoCuries/liter(4 pCi/L), Buyer accepts the Property and agrees to the RELEASE in paragraph 27 of this Agreement.

        2.   If the written test report reveals the presence of radon at or exceeding 0.02 working levels or 4 picoCuries/liter (4 pCi/L), Buyer will proceed under one of the following options as listed in paragraph 10 within the Contingency Period.

            __   Option 1

            __   Option 2

4. STAUTS OF WATER

    (A) Seller represents that the Property is served by:

        __   Public Water

        __   On-site Water

        __   Community Water

        __   None

        __ _____

    (B) WATER SERVICE INSPECTION CONTINGENCY

        __   WAIVED. Buyer has the option to have an inspection of the quality and or quantity of the water system for the Property. BUYER WAIVES THIS OPTION and agrees to the RELEASE in paragraph 27 of this Agreement.

        __   ELECTED. Contingency Period ___ days (15 if not specified) from the Execution Date of this Agreement.

Figure 6:18 Sample Sales Contract

1. Within the Contingency Period, Buyer, at Buyer's expense, may obtain an inspection of the quality and/or quantity of the water system from a properly licensed or otherwise qualified water/well testing company.
2. If required by the inspection company, Seller, at Seller's expense, will locate and provide access to the on-site (or individual) water system. Seller also agrees to restore the Property, at Seller's expense, prior to settlement.
3. If Buyer is not satisfied with the condition of the water system as stated in the written inspection report(s), Buyer will proceed under one of the following options as listed in paragraph 10 within the Contingency Period:
   __ Option 1
   __ Option 2

(C) In the event any notices (including violations) and/or assessments are received after Seller has signed this Agreement and before settlement, Seller will provide a copy of the notices and/or assessments to Buyer and will notify Buyer in writing within ___ days after receiving the notices and/or assessments that seller will:
1. Fully comply with the notices and/or assessments at Seller's expense before settlement. If Seller fully complies with the notices and/or assessments, Buyer accepts the Property and agrees to the RELEASE in paragraph 27 of this Agreement OR
2. Not comply with the notices and/or assessments. If Seller chooses not to comply with the notices and/or assessments, or fails within the time given to notify Buyer whether Seller will comply, Buyer will notify Seller in writing within ___ days that Buyer will:
   a. Comply with the notices and/or assessments at Buyer's expense, accept the Property, and agree to the RELEASE in paragraph 27 of this Agreement OR
   b. Terminate this Agreement by written notice to Seller, with all deposit monies returned to Buyer according to the terms of paragraph 30 of this Agreement.
   If Buyer fails to respond within the time stated in paragraph 18 (C) (2) or fails to terminate this Agreement by written notice to the Seller within that time, Buyer will accept the Property and agree to the RELEASE in paragraph 27 of this Agre

(D) If required by law, within ___ DAYS From the Execution Date of this Agreement, but in no case later than 15 days prior to settlement, Seller will order at Seller's expense a certification from the appropriate municipal department(s) disclosing notice of any uncorrected violations of zoning, housing, building, safety, or fire ordinances and/or a certificate permitting occupancy of the Property. If Buyer receives notice of any required repairs/improvements, Buyer will promptly deliver a copy of the notice to the Seller.
1. Within ___ DAYS of receiving notice form the municipality that repairs/improvements are required, Seller will notify Buyer in writing that the Seller will:
   a. Make the required repairs/improvements to the satisfaction of the municipality. If Seller makes the required repairs/improvements, Buyer accepts the Property and agrees to the RELEASE in paragraph 27 of this Agreement OR
   b. Not make the required repairs/improvements. If Seller chooses not to make the required repairs/improvements, Buyer will notify Seller in writing within ___ DAYS that Buyer will:
      (1) Make the repairs/improvements at Buyer's expense, with permission and access to the Property given by Seller, which will not be unreasonably withheld, OR
      (2) Terminate this Agreement by written notice to Seller, with all deposit monies returned to Buyer according to the terms of paragraph 30 of this Agreement.
      If Buyer fails to respond within the time stated in paragraph 18 (D) (1) (b) or fails to terminate this Agreement by written notice to Seller within that time, Buyer will accept the Property and agree to the RELEASE in paragraph 27 of this Agreement, and Buyer accepts the responsibility to perform the repairs/improvements according to the terms of the notice provided by the municipality.
2. If Seller denies Buyer permission to make the required repairs/improvements, or does not provide Buyer access before settlement to make the required repairs/improvements, Buyer may, within ___ DAYS, terminate this Agreement by written notice to Seller, with all deposit monies returned to Buyer according to paragraph 30 of this Agreement
3. If repairs/improvements are required and Seller fails to provide a copy of the notice to Buyer as required in paragraph 18 (D), Seller will perform all repairs/improvements as required by the notice at Seller's expense. Paragraph 18(D)(3) will survive settlement.

19. TITLE, SURVEYS & COSTS
(A) The Property will be conveyed with good and marketable title as is insurable by a reputable title company at the regular rates, free and clear of all liens, encumbrances, and easements, EXCEPTING HOWEVER the following: existing deed restrictions; historic preservation restrictions or ordinances; building restrictions; ordinances; easements of roads; easements visible upon the ground; easements of record; and privileges or rights of public service companies, if any.
(B) Buyer will pay for the following: (1) Title search, title insurance and/or mechanics' lien insurance, or any fee for cancellation; (2) Flood insurance, fire insurance with extended coverage, mine subsidence insurance, or any fee for cancellation; (3) Appraisal fees and charges paid in advance to mortgage lender(s); (4) Buyer's customary settlement costs and accruals.
(C) Any survey or surveys required by the title insurance company or abstracting attorney for preparing an adequate legal description of the Property (or the correction thereof) will be obtained and paid for by Seller. Any survey or surveys desired by Buyer or required by the mortgage lender will be obtained and paid for by Buyer.
(D) If Seller is unable to give a good and marketable title and such as is insurable by a reputable title insurance company at the regular rates, as specified in paragraph 19 (A), Buyer will:
1. Accept the Property with such title as Seller can give, with no change to the purchase price, and agree to the RELEASE in paragraph 27 of this Agreement, OR

Figure 6:19 Sample Sales Contract

STATEMENT OF ESTIMATED SELLER'S COSTS

Date Prepared   Sellers

Prepared By   Property

The following estimate is given so that the Sellers will understand approximately what costs will be deducted from the proceeds of the sale at the time of settlement.

		Sales Price	$
1.)	Deed Preparation		$
2.)	Settlement Fee		$
3.)	State ____% Transfer Tax		$
4.)	Local ____% Transfer Tax		$
5.)	Broker Fee		$
Total Cost To Seller			$
Net Amount To Seller			$

I/We understand that this is only an estimate of My/Our costs relative to the sale of _____ No consideration has been given for Pro-Rated Taxes, Water and Sewage, or Balance Due on Mortgage if any. I/We understand that this in only an estimate of my/our costs and acknowledge receipt of a copy of the statement of Estimated Seller's Costs.

Figure 6:6 Statement of Estimated Sellers Costs Example

Parcel ID No.

File No.

This Indenture, made the _____ day of _____, 20 _____

Between

                                              (hereinafter called Grantor) of the one part and

                                              (hereinafter called Grantee) of the other part.

Witnesseth, that the said Grantor for and in consideration of _____ dollars ($_____) lawful money of the United States of America, unto him well and truly paid by the said Grantee, at or before the sealing and delivery hereof, the receipt whereof is hereby acknowledged, has granted, bargained, and sold, released, and confirmed, and by these presents does grant, bargain and sell, release and confirm unto the said Grantee, as the sole owner.

All that certain lot or piece of ground situate in _____ _____ being lot No _____, Page _____ being more fully described as follows

       Bounded on the northwest by Pine street, on the Southwest by lot No. 200-17-21B (now or formerly of Mr. Jones et al); fronting twenty-five (25) feet on the Southeast side of First Avenue, between 3rd and 4th Streets and extending back at an equal width to a depth of One Hundred Twenty (120) feet.

       Being known and numbered as Premises 322 First Avenue.

       Being further identified as This County Tax Parcel Number 200-17-19A

       Also ALL those certain lots or pieces of ground situate in This County in the City of Nod, County of There, and State of Freedom.

Figure 8:1 Sample General Warranty Deed Page 1

Together with all and singular the buildings and improvements, ways, streets, alleys, driveways, passages, waters, water-courses, rights, liberties, privileges, hereditaments, and appurtenances whatsoever unto the hereby granted premises belonging or in anywise appertaining, and the revisions and remainders, rents, issues, and profits thereof; and all the estate, right, title, interest, property, claim and demand whatsoever of him, the said grantor, as well at the laws in equity, of, in and to the same.

To have and to hold the said lot or piece of ground described above, with the buildings and improvements thereon erected, hereditaments and premises hereby granted, or mentioned and intended so to be, with the appurtenances, unto the said Grantee, here heirs and assigns, to and for the only property use and behoof of the said Grantee, her heirs and assigns, forever.

And the said Grantor, for herself and her heirs, executors and administrators, does, by these presents, covenant, grant and agree, to and with the said Grantee, her heirs and assigns, that he, the said Grantor, and his heirs, and against all and every other person and persons whosoever lawfully claiming or to claim the same or any part thereof, by, from or under him, her, it, or any of them shall and will.

Warrant and Forever Defend

In Witness Whereof, the party of the first part has hereunto set his hand and seal. Dated the day and year first above written.

      Sealed and Delivered
      IN THE PRESENCE OF US:

{Seal

Figure 8:2 Sample Form – Deed Page 2

Parcel ID No.

File No.

JUDIICAL SALE IN CONNECTION WITH THE TAX SALE OF 20___

DEED

OF

TAX CLAIM BUREAU OF ANY COUNTY, ANYWHERE

Made the _____ day of _____, Two Thousand _____ (20_＿_)

Between the TAX CLAIM BUREAU OF _____ COUNTY (the latter a subdivision of   the City of _____ with a seat of government in the Borough of   _____ County of _____ and Commonwealth of _____) as constituted and created by virtue of the provisions of the Act   of Assembly approved the 7th day of July, 1947, P.L. 1368 (72 PS 5860.101) and known as the   "Real Estate Tax Sale Law" as supplemented and amended, as trustee for

Owner or reputed owners, herein designated as Grantor of Party of the First Part;

AND

of the City of _____, County of _____, and Commonwealth   or State of _____, herein designated as Grantee or Party of the   Second Part;

Witnesseth THAT WHEREAS, the real estate hereinafter identified was exposed to the Tax Sale   duly held by the First Party on the ____ day of _____, 20 ___, as continued, adjourned, or readjourned, under and by virtue of the provisions of the Act of Assembly hereinbefore identified and the upset price was not bid by anyone is such Sale; and

WITNESSETH, THAT WHEREAS, by proceedings filed to No. _____ a Decree of the Court of Common Please of _____ County, was entered directing that said property be sold at a subsequent date fixed by the Court, free and clear of all tax and municipal claims, mortgages, liens, charges, and estates, of whatsoever kind, with the purchaser at said sale to have an absolute title to said property, free and clear of the claims aforesaid;

AND WHEREAS, the Second Party became the purchaser, (or is the heir or assignee of said purchaser) of said real estate at the Judicial Sale held by the First Party on the _____ day of _____ A.D. 20 ___, as continued, adjourned, or readjourned, under and by virtue of the provisions of the Act of Assembly hereinbefore identified.

NOW, THEREFORE, WITNESSETH, that under and in pursuance of the Act of Assembly aforesaid and the Order of Court entered in connection, therewith, and for and in consideration of $_____ _____ Dollars, in hand paid, the receipt of which is herewith acknowledged, (being the price bid at said Judicial Sale), the receipt of which is herewith acknowledged, (being the price bid at said Judicial Sale), the Grantor or Party of the First Part, under and by virtue of the Act of Assembly aforesaid as Trustee for the owner or reputed owner of said Real

Estate, does hereby grant, bargain, sell, assign, and release, in fee simple, unto the said Grantee or Party of the Second Part, their heirs, successors, and assigns,

ALL

      Control # 060-0027

      Map # 0800-21-17B

For chain of title see DBV 1128 page 116

All taxes up to and including 20____ County and Township were in sale.

Realty transfer tax is $_____ for 1% Local and $_____ for 1% State, based on the Common Level Ratio Factor at the time of the sale, which was 11.91%.

TO the end that said purchaser shall take and hold an absolute title to the said property free and clear of all tax and municipal claims, mortgages, liens, charges, and estates of whatsoever kind, except ground rent separately taxed.

TO HAVE AND TO HOLD the said premises, without warranty of any kind or nature, unto the said Party of the Second Part, their heirs, successors, and assigns forever.

IN WITNESS WHEREOF, the said Party of the First Part set its hand and seal the day and year aforesaid.

Figure 7:4 Sample Tax Deed

QUITCLAIM DEED

FOR A VALUABLE CONDIERATION.   HEREBY QUITCLAIM to:

The real property in the County of _____, State of _____ described as

Witness my hand this _____ day of _____, 20 ____.

_____   _____

State of   }   Witness my hand and official seal:
                                            }
County of   }
On _____, 20____   _____
Before me, the undersigned, a Notary Public   Notary Public in and for Said County
and State
and for said County and State personally
appeared   NOTARY SEAL

Proved to me on the basis of satisfactory
evidence to be the person whose name is (are)
sub-scribed to the instrument and
acknowledge that

executed the same.

Figure 7:5 Sample Quit Claim Deed

TYPE OF OWNERSHIP	NUMBER OR INDIVIDUALS	AMOUNT OF INTEREST	SIGNATURES FOR SALE
Joint Tenancy	Two or more people	Equal interest according to contract	Each individual owner may sell their interest without the consent of the other parties. All parties must sign for a full transfer of ownership.
Tenancy in Common	Two or more people	Equal or unequal interest	Each individual owner may sell their interest without the consent of the other parties.
Community Property / Tenancy by the entirety	Ownership between spouses only	Equal interest	The property may only be sold with the partners consent and both signatures are required.
Sole Ownership	One Person	Undivided / sole interest	Only the single owner's signature is required.

AGREEMENT TO CHANGE TITLE FROM JOINT TENANCY TO COMMUNITY PROPERTY

1. PARTIES:

Parties to this agreement are _____

and _____.

2. RECITALS:

a) The parties hereto are husband and wife, residing in the County of _____
    State of _____.

b) They have heretofore held property in their common or separate names, and may
    hereafter do so.

c) They hold portions of their property in joint tenancy only as a matter of convenience or
    transfer.

d) This agreement is entered into with the full knowledge on the part of each party of the
    extent and probable value of all of the property and estate of the community, and of the
    separate and joint property of each other, ownership of which would be conferred by law
    on each of them in the event of the termination of their relationship by death or
    otherwise.

e) It is the express intent of the parties hereto that all their common properties are and shall
    be their community property.

3. AGREEMENT THAT ALL PROPERTY SHALL BE COMMUNITY

Each party hereby releases all of his or her separate rights in and to any and all property,
real or personal and wherever situated, which either party now owns or has an interest in,
and each party agrees that all property or interest therein owned heretofore or presently or
hereafter acquired by either from common funds shall be deemed to be community
property of the parties hereto, whether held in their separate names, as joint tenants, as
tenants in common, or in any other legal form. The parties understand that this
agreement will automatically, without other formality, transfer to the other a one-half
interest in any separate property now owned and that such transfer could constitute a
taxable gift under Federal and State law.

4. AGREEMENT MODIFIABLE IN WRITING ONLY:

This agreement shall not be modified except in writing signed by both parties, or by the
mutual written surrender or abandonment of their said community interest in accordance
with the laws of said State pertaining to the management of community property, or by
the termination of their marriage by death or otherwise.

Figure 9:2 Sample Tenancy Change Form

Loan#	LENDER'S CLOSING INSTRUCTIONS	Date

Borrower

Property Address:

Return Original Signed Documents to Lender:

Loan Terms

Loan Amount:

Interest Rate:

Term

Loan Type:

Loan Purpose:

___ 1st MTG or ___ 2nd MTG

Estimated Funding Date

Settlement Agent

Title Company

Phone:	Phone:
Fax:	Fax:
Email:	Email:
Attn:	Attn:
Closing #:	Order #:

1. LOAN DISBURSEMENTS

FEE		POC	BUYER	SELLER	LENDER	OTHER	HUD-1 PAYABLE TO
801	Origination Points						
802	Lender Discount Pints						
803	Lender Appraisal Fee to						
804	Lender Credit Report to						
805	Lender Inspection						
806	Mortgage Insurance Ap Fee						
807	Assumption Fee						
808							
809							
810	Administration Fee to						
811	Application Fee to						
812	Processing Fee to						
813	Wire Transfer Fee to						

814 Underwriting Fee to

815 Flood Cert to

816 Tax Service to

817 Buydown Fee to

818

819

820

821

901 Prepaid Int (days @ /day)

902 PMI Premium

903 Property Insurance

904 Flood Insurance

905 VA Funding Fee

906

1001 Property Ins (pmts @ /mth)

1002 Mortgage Ins (pmts @ /mth)

1003 City Taxes (pmts @ /mth)

1004 County Tax (pmts @ /mth)

1005 Annual Asmnt (pmts @ /mth)

1006 Flood Ins (pmts @ /mth)

1007 School Taxes (pmts @ /mth)

1008 (pmts @ /mth)

1009 Aggregate Adjustment

1101 Settlement or Closing Fee

1102 Abstract or Title Search

1103 Title Examination

1104 Title Ins Binder

1105 Document Prep fee

1106 Notary Fee

1107 Attorney's Fee

1108 Title Insurance

1111

1112

1113

1201 Recording Fees

1202 City Taxes & Stamps

1203 State Taxes & Stamps

1204

1205

1301 Survey

1302 Pest Inspection

1303 Final Inspection to

1304

1305 Review Appraiser to

703 Commission Paid At Settlement

Totals

a)   Other than the fees listed, no other fees or charges may be charged without prior approval from Lender.

b)   Additional compensation of $ _____ will be paid by Lender to _____ . This amount is not deducted from _____ the principal balance of the loan. The compensation must show on HUD-1 as "Broker Fee paid by Lender POC"

c)   Unless notified otherwise by Lender, we will remit our wire to you in the amount of the loan, less fees paid to Lender. The "Broker Fee paid   by Lender POC" will be included in the wire when applicable.

2.   PAYOFFS   COMPANY   ACCOUNT # _____   AMT. TO BE PAID

3.   REQUIREMENTS: The documents or requirements indicated below must be executed or satisfied. You are responsible to ensure that each borrower receives two signed, dated and fully completed copies of the NOTICE OF RIGHT TO CANCEL (if applicable) and one copy of the FEDERAL TRUTH-IN-LENDING DISCLOSURE STATEMENT.

__ Deed/Mortgage with applicable riders   __ Note with Applicable Addendums

__ Federal Truth-In-Lending Disclosure Statement   __ Original Application to be signed

__ Power of attorney (original)   __ Request for taxpayer's ID (IRS W-9)

__ Right to cancel notice   __ Typed application to be signed

__ Certified proof of funds to close   __ Itemization of amount financed

__ Tax Certification form   __ Grant/Warranty Deed

__

__

__

4.   FUNDING CONDITIONS: The following approval conditions remain outstanding. Borrower is being allowed to sign documents subject to Lender's receipt and approval of these conditions. You are not authorized to disburse funds until Lender has approved the following:

HUD to be faxed to   for review and approval

Need certified copy of warranty deed (for CA grant deed) signed by seller(s)

Need copy of certified funds buyer bring for closing costs (CAN'T DISBURSE FUNDS WITHOUT IT)

Need evidence of hazard insurance, paid for one year

All taxes to be current at close

All signed docs to be returned to us immediately after signing in return fed-ex envelope provided

5. In connection with this loan, we enclose the necessary documents requiring signature and acknowledgement where applicable. All loan documents must be executed exactly as the names are shown below the signature lines. No alterations or erasures to these documents are permitted without our approval.

   a. A Specific Power of Attorney cannot execute documents, without prior approval from Lender. A General Power of Attorney will not be accepted. Examples of POA signatures

      John Jones by Nancy Jones as Attorney in fact. Initials should read as JJ by NJ as A.I.F.

      Nancy Jones as Attorney in fact for John Jones. Initials should read NJ as A.I.F. for JJ

6. In addition to the above, return the following:

   b. Original HUD-1 settlement statement with all payees as shown on these instructions. Sellers closing cost credits are limited to non-recurring costs only, and are further limited to 6% (3% for TX home equity) of sales price of the home. Credit   can't exceed the actual non-recurring costs. Examples of recurring closing costs are: odd days interest, hazard, flood,   windstorm insurance premiums, property taxes, HOA dues. Broker credits must also be included in this 6% credit figure.

   c. Certified copy of all checks for balance due at closing from borrower. Must be certified check, no cash deposits allowed unless approved by   lender.

   d. 2 Certified copies of signed, notarized Deed of Trust/Mortgage and Riders

   e. Certified copy of second Deed of Trust/Mortgage and Note in the amount of $, interest rate   %, monthly payment $ and term of

   f. Certified copy of any Grant/Warranty Deed from seller (seller to match Preliminary Title Report), inter-spousal transfer deeds or other   quitclaims being executed for this transaction.

   g. Original copy of any and all duly executed Settlement Closing Instructions and amendments thereto, including correct lender, rate and terms.

   h. Copy of borrower's valid photo identification used at closing.

7. We require a standard ALTA Policy within 15 days from the funding of this loan.

   SHORT FORM POLICES ARE NOT ALLOWED

   Individual title reports required for first and second mortgages. The ALTA Policy must contain a Plat Map or survey Endorsements 100 and Form 8.1 as required without deletion, 116, 115, 116.2 (if subject property is a Condominium Estate), 115.2 (if the subject property is a Planned Unit Development), and Special Endorsements:
   With liability in the amount of our loan(s) on the subject property, subject only to:

   a) General and special taxes and assessments not yet due (all such taxes and assessments, which are due as of the settlement date must be paid   current at closing) and

   b) Items   as shown on the preliminary report of title No.   date

8. Secondary financing in the amount of $ (none if left blank) has been approved. The total consideration in this transaction except for our loan(s) proceeds and any permitted secondary financing, must be paid in cash. Do not record or disburse funds if you have

knowledge or reason to suspect the borrower intends to obtain secondary financing to purchase the subject property other than as permitted herein.

Additionally, you are instructed not to record or disburse funds if you have knowledge or reason to suspect that the purchase price of the subject property is not $ or that any portion of the purchase price is being paid other than with certified funds without prior written authorization from us. No other subordinate financing is allowed without prior written approval from Lender.

9.   It is strictly forbidden to allow a Broker, or Broker affiliate company to close our transaction.

10. All closing documents should be executed in BLUE INK.

11. If State requirements exist, a Non borrower must execute a Deed of Trust/Mortgage, Riders, Federal Truth-In-Lending Disclosure Statement, Itemization of Amount Financed, Notice of Right to Cancel, Warranty and Compliance Agreement, Signature Affidavit and AKA Statement, and Correction Agreement Limited Power of Attorney. A valid photo I.D. must also be provided.

12. ALL TRANSACTIONS: Prior to the disbursement of any funds the closing agent must fax to the Lender the documents listed below for their review and approval. Owner occupied refinance transactions may not be disbursed prior to the day following the Rescission expiration date provided to the borrowers on the notice of right to cancel.

   Signature page of: Note and Addendums, Deed of Trust/Mortgage and Riders

   Executed Grant/Warranty Deed witnessed and notarized, if applicable

   Copy of any certified check(s) for funds to close. Remitter must be the borrower's name and drawn on the borrower's bank

   Any specific closing conditions outlined above under FUNDING CONDITIONS

   Executed final HUD-1 statement

   Federal Truth-in-Lending Statement

   Notice of Right to Cancel, if applicable

   Power of Attorney, if applicable

13. We reserve the right to withdraw these instructions and enclosures if this loan is not closed on or before
   if for any reason this loan does not close, return all documents, together with these instructions, to the Lender and notify Lender immediately. We will incur no expense in the closing of this transaction unless otherwise noted in these instructions.

10:1 Example – Lender's Closing Instructions

MAILING ADDRESS CONFIRMATION / PAYMENT LETTER

From:

Re: Loan #   *** IMPORTANT, PLEASE READ THROUGHOULY ***

        Property Address

To:

Dear Homeowner:

A.   All mortgage servicing correspondence will be mailed to the above referenced property address. In order to ensure proper receipt of all mortgage servicing notifications (i.e. monthly statement, Q&A booklets, etc.) please indicate the correct mailing address if it is different from the property address. The address to mail payments and the phone number to call for customer service are listed below.

      Please indicate (X):

      ( )   The property address is correct as referenced above and should be used for correspondence.

      ( )   The proper mailing address is: _____

                                             _____

B.   The monthly payments on the above loan are to begin on   , and will continue monthly until

      Your monthly payment will consist of the following:

      MONTHLY PAYMENT ……………………………………………..$ _____

      MMI/PMI INSRUANCE ……………………………………….. _____

      RESERVE FOR COUNTY TAXES ………………………………. _____

      RESERVE FOR HAXARD INSURANCE………………………… _____

      RESERVE FOR FLOOD INSURANCE…………………………. _____

      RESERVE FOR CITY TAXES……………………………………._____

      RESERVE FOR ANNUAL ASSESSMENT……………………._____

      RESERVE FOR SCHOOL TAXES…………………………….._____

_____ ...._____

TOTAL MONTHLY PAYMENTS..........$_____

*** Please be aware that if you have an impound account, you may see a change in your initial monthly payment figure due to information available after the closing of your loan.

                    Engages the services of   as its servicer. You will be receiving a billing notice from   within two weeks of your loan funding.   has the right to collect your payments and this in no way affects the terms and conditions of the mortgage instruments, other than the terms directly related to the servicing of your loan. If you do not receive a payment booklet or have other questions about the servicing of your loan, please call:

Please send your payments to:

Any correspondence, or calls, in reference to your loan, please refer to the above loan number. However, your loan number will be changed for servicing purposes.

Copy received and acknowledged.

Figure 10:10 Sample Mailing Address Confirmation

LOAN ASSUMPTION ADDENDUM

TO CONTRACT CONCERNING THE PROPERTY AT: (Address of Property)

_____

A.   CREDIT DOCUMENTATION:

Within _____ days after the effective date of this contract,

Purchaser shall deliver to Seller the following: (check all applicable items

_____ Credit report

_____ Verification of employment, including salary

_____ Verification of funds on deposit in financial institutions

_____ Current financial statement to establish Purchaser's creditworthiness

_____ Other: _____

Purchaser hereby authorizes any credit-reporting agency to furnish to Seller at Purchaser's sole expense copies of Purchaser's credit reports.
_____ Signature

B.   CREDIT APPROVAL: If Purchaser's documentation is not delivered within the specified time, Seller may terminate this contract by notice to Purchaser within 7 days after expiration of the time for delivery, and the earnest money will be paid to Seller.

If the documentation is timely delivered, and Seller determines in Seller's sole discretion that Purchaser's credit is unacceptable, Seller may terminate this contract by notice to Purchaser   within 7 days after expiration of the time for delivery and the earnest money will be refunded to Purchaser.

If Seller does not terminate this contract, Seller will be deemed to have accepted Purchaser's credit.

C.   ASSUMPTION:

_____ (1)The unpaid principal balance of a first lien promissory note payable to which unpaid balance at closing will be $_____. The total current monthly payment including principal, interest and any reserve deposits is

$_____. Purchaser's initial payment will be the first payment due after closing.

_____ (2) The unpaid principal balance of a second lien promissory note payable to which unpaid balance at closing will be $_____. The total current monthly payment including principal, interest and any reserve deposits is $_____. Purchaser's initial payment will be the first payment due after closing.

Purchaser's assumption of an existing note includes all obligations imposed by the deed of trust   securing the note. If the unpaid principal balance(s) of any assumed loan(s) as of the Closing Date varies from the loan balance(s) stated above, the (check only one

D.   Cash payable at closing

Sales Price will be adjusted by the amount of any variance; provided, if the total principal balance of all assumed loans varies in an amount greater than $350.00 at closing, either party may terminate this contract and the earnest money will be refunded to Purchaser unless the other party elects to eliminate the excess in the variance by an appropriate adjustment at closing.   Purchaser may terminate this contract and the earnest money will be refunded to Purchaser if the note holder requires

1.   payment of an assumption fee in excess of $_____ in (A) above or $_____ in (2) above and Seller declines to pay such excess, an increase in the interest rate to more than _____% in (1) above, or _____% in (B) above, any other modification of the loan documents, or consent to the assumption of the loan and fails to consent.

2.   An appropriate instrument authorized within the state, typically either

(A) a mortgage or

(B) Vendor's and deed of trust liens,

To secure the assumption will be required, and it will automatically be released on execution and delivery of a release by note holder. If Seller is released from liability on any assumed note, the instrument securing the assumption will not be required. If note holder maintains an escrow account, the escrow account must be transferred to Purchaser without any deficiency. Purchaser shall reimburse Seller for the amount in the transferred accounts.

E.   NOTICE TO PURCHASER: The monthly payments, interest rates or other terms of some loans may be adjusted by the note holder at or after closing. If you are concerned about the possibility of future adjustments, do not sign the contract without examining the notes and the instrument securing the note.

F.   NOTICE TO SELLER: Your liability to pay the note assumed by Purchaser will continue unless you obtain a release of liability from the note holder. If you are concerned about future liability, you should use a Release of Liability Addendum.

PURCHASER:

_____   _____
Date   Purchaser Signature

                                                _____
                                                Printed Name

SELLER:

_____   _____
Date   Seller Signature

                                                _____
                                                Printed Name

Figure 10-27 Sample Assumption Addendum

MORTGAGE ASSUMPTION AGREEMENT

THIS MORTGAGE ASSUMPTION AGREEMENT (hereinafter referred to as the "Agreement") made and
entered into as of this __ day of _____, 20__, by and between
_____, of
_____, (hereinafter referred to as the
"Lender") and _____, of
_____ (hereinafter referred to as "Borrower").

W I T N E S S E T H:

WHEREAS, Lender is the holder and owner of the following documents (hereinafter sometimes collectively referred to as the "Loan Documents"):

1.   Mortgage Note dated _____, in the original principal face amount of _____ DOLLARS ($_____) executed and delivered by _____ (hereinafter referred to as the "Original Borrower" in favor of Lender   (hereinafter referred to as the "Note"); and,

2.   Mortgage given by Original Borrower as "Mortgagor" to Lender as "Mortgagee" dated _____, which Mortgage is recorded on the Public Records of _____ County, _____ at O.R. Book __, Page __ (hereinafter referred to as the "Mortgage"), and which   Mortgage encumbers the real property as described therein; and,

WHEREAS, the Original Borrower is desirous of conveying the property encumbered by the Mortgage, (hereinafter referred to as the "Property") to Borrower; and,

WHEREAS, the Borrower desires to receive said Property and formally assume the Mortgage and perform all of the covenants and conditions contained in the Mortgage Note, the Mortgage and all other Loan Documents as partial consideration for its purchase of the Property and as consideration for the Lender's willingness to consent to the sale of the Property which is encumbered by the Loan Documents; and,

WHEREAS, the Mortgage expressly prohibits the conveyance of the Property without the express written consent of the Lender; and,

WHEREAS, the Lender is unwilling to give its consent to the transfer of the Property to the Borrower unless the Borrower shall assume all of the obligations heretofore imposed by the Loan Documents upon the Original Borrower;

NOW, THEREFORE, for and in consideration of the sum of _____ DOLLARS ($_____) and in consideration of the Premises and of the mutual covenants contained herein, and for other good and valuable considerations, the receipt and sufficiency of which are hereby acknowledged by the parties, the parties hereto agree as follows:

1.   Assumption. Borrower expressly assumes the Loan Documents, agrees to perform all covenants, conditions, duties and obligations contained therein, and agrees to pay the Note and the obligations evidenced thereby in a prompt and timely manner in accordance with the terms thereof.

2.   Consent to Conveyance. Lender hereby consents to the transfer of the Property to the Borrower, but the Lender expressly reserves the right to withhold its consent to any future sale or transfer of the Property, as provided for in the Mortgage.

3.   Warranties and Representations. Borrower affirms warrants, represents and covenants that Borrower has neither defenses nor rights of set-off against Lender or against the payment, collection or enforcement of the indebtedness evidenced by the Note and secured by the Mortgage and owed to Lender. Borrower further warrants and represents as follows:

      a. Borrower has done no acts nor omitted to do any act which might prevent Lender from, or limit Lender in, acting upon or under any of the provisions herein, in the Mortgage, in the Note or any other Loan Documents

      b. Borrower is not prohibited under any other agreement with any other person or any judgment or decree, from the execution and delivery of this Agreement, the performance of each and every covenant hereunder or under the Mortgage, Note or any other Loan Documents

      c. No action has been brought or threatened which would in any way interfere with the right of Borrower to execute this Agreement and perform all of Borrower's obligations contained herein, in the Note, in the Mortgage, or in any other Loan Document

      d. All financial statements of Borrower and Guarantors, if any, are true and correct in all respects, fairly present the respective financial conditions of the subjects thereof, as of the respective dates thereof and no material adverse change has occurred that would affect Borrower's or Guarantors', if any, ability to repay the indebtedness evidenced by the Note and   secured by the Mortgage

e. Borrower is duly formed, validly existing and in good standing under the laws of the State of _____ and has full power and authority to consummate the transactions contemplated under this Agreement.

4. Acknowledgements. Borrower acknowledges that:

    a. The Loan Documents are in full force and effect; and,

    b. The principal balance of the loan as represented by the aforesaid Note as of the date of this Agreement is _____ DOLLARS ($_____) and principal and interest are unconditionally due and owing to the Lender as provided in the Note.

5. Costs. Borrower shall pay all costs of the assumption made hereby, to include without limitation, attorneys' fees and recording costs, as well as the cost of an endorsement to Lender's title insurance policy insuring the lien of the Mortgage after the recording of this Agreement. Such costs shall be due at closing hereunder and the payment thereof shall be a condition precedent to Lender's consent to the transfer of the Property to Borrower. In the event that it is determined that additional costs relating to this transaction are due, Borrower agrees to pay such costs immediately upon demand.

6. Assumption Fee. In consideration of Lender's consenting to the conveyance of the Property to the Borrower, Lender is entitled to, and has earned, an assumption fee in the amount of __ percent (___%) of the original principal face amount of the indebtedness evidenced by the Note. Said fee shall be due and payable upon the execution and delivery of this Agreement. Borrower hereby agrees and acknowledges that said fee is being charged solely for costs relating to the assumption of the Mortgage and not as interest for the forbearance or use of money.

7. Recordation. The recording of this Agreement on the Public Records shall evidence the closing of the transaction described herein.

8. Paragraph Headings. The paragraph headings used herein are for convenience of reference only and shall not be used in the interpretation or construction hereof.

9. Governing Law. This Agreement shall be governed, interpreted and construed by, through and under the laws of the State of _____.

10. Time of the Essence. Time is of the essence of this Agreement.

11. Attorneys' Fees. All costs incurred by Lender in enforcing this Agreement and in collection of sums due Lender from Borrower, to include, without limitation, reasonable attorneys' fees through all trials, appeals, and proceedings, to include,

without limitation, any proceedings pursuant to the bankruptcy laws of the United States and any arbitration proceedings, shall be paid by Borrower.

12.   Binding Effect. This Agreement shall inure to the benefit of and be binding upon the parties hereto as well as their successors and assigns, heirs and personal representatives.

IN WITNESS WHEREOF, the parties hereto have duly executed this Agreement as follows:

As to Lender this ___ day of _____, 20_____.

"LENDER"   WITNESSES:

_____   _____

As to Borrower this day of _____, 20_____.

"BORROWER"   WITNESSES:

_____   _____

Figure 10.30 Sample Assumption Agreement

ITEMIZATION OF AMOUNT FINANCED

Borrower   Creditor:

Loan Number: Date:

Property Address: Term:

                                            Rate:

                                            LTV:

Listed below is the ITEMIZATION OF AMOUNT FINANCED.

Existing Lien: $

Loan Amount $

ITEMIZATION OF PRPAID FINANCE CHARGES:

    -- Origination Points   to LENDER

    -- Lender Discount Points   to LENDER

    -- Administration Fee to LENDER

    -- Prepaid Interest for

    -- Settlement or Closing Fee to

        TOTAL PREPAID FINANCE CHARGE: $

        AMOUNT FINANCED: $

OTHER SETTLEMENT CHARGES:

AMOUNTS PAID TO OTHERS ON YOUR
BEHALF BY CREDITOR

-- Lender Appraisal Fee to

-- Abstract or Title Search to

-- Notary Fee to

-- Title Insurance to

-- Recording Fee (Deed: $)

TOTAL OTHER SETTLEMENT CHARGE: $_____

LOAN PROCEEDS: $_____

FEES PAID BY LENDER

TOTAL FEES PAID BY LENDER: $_____

I (We) hereby acknowledge that I (we) have received and read a completed copy of the HUD Special Information Booklet "Settlement Cost", unless the loan being applied is for refinancing the property.

If for any reason the loan I (we) have applied for does not close, and if permitted by applicable law, I (we) agree to reimburse the lender for any and all costs incurred to process my (our) application including, but not limited to: appraisal, survey, and title insurance.

Figure 11:1 Sample Itemization of Amount Financed

CORRECTION AGREEMENT
LIMITED POWER OF ATTORNEY

On   , the undersigned Borrower(s), for and in consideration of the approval, closing and funding of their mortgage loan (No.   ) hereby grant   as settlement agent and/or   as Lender limited power of attorney to correct and/or execute or initial all typographical or clerical errors discovered in any or all of the closing documentation required to be executed by the undersigned at settlement. In the even this limited power of attorney is exercised, the undersigned will be notified and receive a copy of the document executed or initialed on their behalf.

THIS LIMITED POWER OF ATTORNEY MAY NOT BE USED TO INCREASE THE INTERST RATE (NOR THE MARGIN OR INDEX FOR VARIABLE RATE LOANS) THE UNDERSIGNED IS PAYING, INCREASE THE TERM OF THE UDNERSIGNED'S LOAN, INCREASE THE UDNERSIGNED'S OUTSTANDING PRINCIPAL BALANCE OR INCREASE THE UNDERSIGNED'S MONTHLY PRINCIPAL AND INTEREST PAYMENTS. Any of these specified changes must be executed directly by the undersigned.

This Limited Power of Attorney shall automatically terminate 180 days from the closing date of the undersigned's mortgage loan.

Figure 11:2 Sample Correction Agreement

Date:

Lender:

Borrower(s):

Loan Number:

Property Address:

WARRANTY AND COMPLIANCE AGREEMENT

In order to induce the lender to make the above loan and in consideration thereof, the undersigned borrower(s):

1.   Warrants and represents to the lender that all information it or its agents have provided to the lender, including without limitation all information contained in the loan application and all documents associated therewith, is true and accurate in all respects as of the date below. In making this statement, the borrower understands that (a) the lender has relied on the accuracy of such information in its decision to make the loan, and (b) if any such information is inaccurate, the lender or its assignee may foreclose or cancel the loan and pursue other legal remedies, including damages for fraud UNDER THE PROVISIONS OF THE DEED OF TRUST, ITEM 6.

2.   Agrees that if any document evidencing the loan does not correctly or accurately reflect the terms of loans offered by lender in the program under which the undersigned applied including, but not limited to, maturity date, interest rate, refinance options, etc., or is not on a form approved for such program as a result of a mistake or clerical error by lender, whether such mistake or error is mutual or unknown to the undersigned, the undersigned will:

> (a)   execute and/or initial modifications, amendments, or replacement documents as necessary to accurately and correctly reflect the terms of the loan or to ensure the loan is evidenced by the proper documentation; and

> (b)   take such other actions as the lender may reasonably request under the circumstances to correct such mistake or clerical error.

In this connection, the undersigned acknowledges that the lender is a mortgage banker which only makes loans that meet criteria established and/or approved by secondary market investors to whom many of the loans it makes are ultimately sold. The undersigned further understands that the lender only offers loan programs which are approved by such investors or meet their established criteria, that any failure to perform the covenants and promises set forth in this agreement may render a loan unmarketable and thereby result in loss or damage to the lender, and that the undersigned's execution of this agreement and willingness to perform obligations assumed herein are material to the lender's decision to make the loan.

Figure 11:3 Sample Warranty and Compliance Notice

TAX CERTIFICATE

Loan / Contract #

Loan Name:

Loan State

Division:

Address:

Jurisdiction:
Date Added: Date Completed

Refresh Requested: Refresh Completed:

$ Tax Jurisdictions: # Real Parcels:

Parcel #   Control $

YES Delinquent Taxes.

No Exemptions:

Delinquent Amount:

SUMMARY

Jurisdiction	Parcel #	Tax Year	Tax Amount	Due Date*	Paid

* The Due Date listed is the last day to make payment before there are additional penalties and/or interest added to the amount to be paid. In the case of a Discount Due Date, the date is the last day to make payment before the amount to be paid is the next discount amount listed or gross tax listed to be paid.

Figure 11:4 Sample Tax Certificate

BORROWER(S):

PROPERTY ADDRES:

NON IMPOUND NOTICE

I DO UNDERSTAND THAT THE LENDER FOR THIS MORTGAGE WILL NOT IMPOUND FOR REAL ESTATE TAXES AND HOMEOWNERS INSURANCE COVERAGE ON THE ABOVE REFERENCED ACCOUNT.

THE MONTHLY PAYMENT I WILL BE MAKING ONLY COVERS PRINCIPAL AND INTEREST ON THE LOAN.

I AM FULLY RESPONSIBLE TO PAY FOR REAL ESTATE TAXES AND HOMEOWNERS INSURACE POLICY PREMIUMS WHEN THEY BECOME PAYABLE.

Figure 11:5 Sample Non Impound Notice

FEDERAL TRUTH-IN-LENDING DISCLOSURE STATEMENT

Borrower   Creditor

Loan Number   Date

ANNUAL PERCENTAGE RATE The cost of your credit as a yearly rate.	FINANCE CHARGE The dollar amount the credit will cost you.	Amount Financed The amount of credit provided to you or on you behalf	Total of Payments The amount you will have paid after you have made all payments as scheduled

Your payment schedule will be:

No. of Pmts.	Amount of Pmts.	Monthly Pmts. Begin	No. of Pmts	Amount of Pmts.	Monthly Pmts Begin	No. of Pmts.	Amount of Pmts.	Monthly Pmts. Begin

THIS IS AN INTEREST ONLY LOAN, THE FIRST 120 PAYMENTS ARE INTEREST ONLY. THIS LOAN WILL CONTAIN A PREPAYMENT PENALTY FOR 36 MONTHS

USE OF YOUR TELEPHONE,
FACSIMILE AND CELLULAR TELEPHONE NUMBERS

Date:

Borrower(s):   Lender:

Property Address:

Please provide the following information:

Home Telephone Number   (   ) _____   (   ) _____

Work Telephone Number   (   ) _____   (   ) _____

Cellular Telephone Number   (   ) _____   (   ) _____

Facsimile Number   (   ) _____   (   ) _____

Email Address   _____   _____

Name of closest relative   _____   _____

Relative's Telephone   (   ) _____   (   ) _____

By signing below, Borrower agrees that the lender, lender's affiliates, the loan servicer and their respective successors and assigns (collectively "we" may contact you at the telephone numbers and email addresses listed above for any purpose related to the servicing and collection of any loan(s) or line of credit we have made to you. You agree that we may use automated dialing and announcing devices to make such calls and that we may contact you at any telephone, facsimile, cellular telephone number, or email address that we may subsequently obtain.

Figure 11:9 Sample Contact Information Request

CREDIT BUREAU NOTICE TO THE HOME APPLICANT

Empirica

_____

current score   date of score

Key Factors:

Equifax

_____

current score   date of score

Key Factors

Experian

_____

current score   date of score

Key Factors

In connection with your application for a home loan, we must disclose to you the score that a credit bureau distributed to users and in connection with your home loan and the key factors affecting your credit score.

The credit score is a computer generate summary calculated at the time of the request and based on information a credit bureau or lender has on file. The scores are based on data about your credit history and payment patterns. Credit scores are important because they are used to assist the lender in determining whether you will obtain a loan. They may also be used to determine what interest rate may be offered on the mortgage. Credit scores can change over time depending on your conduct, how your credit history and payment patterns change, and how credit-scoring technologies change.

Because the score is based on information in your credit history, it is very important that you review the credit-related information that is being furnished to make sure it is accurate. Credit records may vary from one company to another.

If you have questions about your score or the credit information that is furnished to you, contact the credit bureau at the address and telephone number provided in this notice. The credit bureau generated this score. The credit bureau plays no part in the decision to take action on the loan application and is unable to provide you with specific reasons for the decision on the loan application.

Figure 11:10 Sample Credit Bureau Notice

Lender:/Creditor: Loan No.:

GENERAL AUTHORIZATION AND BORROWER'S CERTIFICATION

The Undersigned certify the following:

1.   I/We have applied for a mortgage loan from Lender. In applying for the loan, I/we completed a loan application containing various information on the purpose of the loan, the amount and source of the down payment, employment and income information, and assets and liabilities. I/We certify that all of the information is true and complete. I/We made no misrepresentations in he loan application or other documents, nor did I/we omit any pertinent information.

2.   I/We understand and agree that in the event the loan is processed under a reduced documentation program, Lender reserves the right to change the mortgage loan review process to a full documentation program. This may include verifying the information provided on the application with the employer and/or financial institution.

3.   I/We fully understand that it is a Federal crime punishable by fine, or imprisonment, or both to knowingly make any false statements when applying for this mortgage, as applicable under the provisions of Title 18, United States Code, Section 1014.

AUTHORIZATION TO RELEASE INFORMATION

1.   I/We have applied for a mortgage loan from Lender. As part of the application process, Lender may verify information contained in my/our loan application and in other documents required in connection with the loan, either before the loan is closed or as part of its quality control program.

2.   I/We authorize you to provide to Lender, and to any investor to whom Lender may sell my mortgage, any and all information and documentation that they request. Such information includes but is not limited to, employment history and income; bank, money market, and similar account balances; credit history; and copies of income tax returns.

3.   Lender or any investor that purchases the mortgage may address this authorization to any party named in the loan application.

4.   A copy of this authorization may be accepted as the original.

5.   Your prompt reply to Lender or the investor that purchased the mortgage is appreciated.

Figure 11:11 Sample General Authorization

ACKNOWLEDGEMENT

STATE OF _____

COUNTY OF _____

On _____ before me, _____, PERSONALLY APPEARED
     (DATE)   NAME, TITLE OFFIER E.G. NOTARY PUBLIC

_____

_____

NAME(S) OF SIGNERS

_____ Personally known to me –or- _ proved to me on the basis of satisfactory evidence to be the person(s) whose name(s) is/are subscribed to the within instrument and acknowledged to me that he/she/ they executed the same in his/her/their authorized capacity(ies), and that by his/her/their signature(s) on the instrument the person(s), or the entity upon behalf of which the person(s) acted, executed the instrument.

    WITNESS my hand and official seal,

                              _____

                              SIGNATURE OF NOTARY

                              MY COMMISSION EXPIRES ON:

Description of Attached Document:

Title to Type of Document: _____

Document Date: _____   Number of Pages: _____

Signors Other Than Named Above: _____

Figure 11:13 Sample Acknowledgement

IDENTIFICATION VALIDATION ACKNOWLEDGEMENT

(This document should be used by the Closing Agent)
(Required when no photo copy of I.D. is available)

Borrower Name(s):

Loan Number:

In accordance with the USA Patriot Act, the following documentation was reviewed to verify the identity of the customer:

___   State issued Driver's License

     B1#_____   Exp Date: _____

     B2#_____   Exp Date: _____

     B3#_____   Exp Date: _____

     B4#_____   Exp Date: _____

___   Passport

     B1#_____   B2#_____

     B3#_____   B4#_____

___   Other (Please describe)

     _____

     B1#_____   B2#_____

     B3#_____   B4#_____

By signing below, the closing agent acknowledges that they have reviewed the above documentation and have verified the identification of the borrowers listed above.

Figure 11:14 Sample Identity Verification

IMPORTANT INFORMATION ABOUT
PROCEDURES FOR YOUR NEW LOAN REQUEST

To help the government fight the funding of terrorism and money laundering activities, Federal law requires all financial institutions to obtain, verify, and record information that identifies each person who opens an account.

What this means for you: When you open an account, we will ask for your name, address, date of birth, business documents, and other information that will allow us to identify you. We may also ask to see your driver's license or other identifying documents.

Figure 11:15 Sample Terrorism Notice

SIGNATURE AFFADAVIT AND AKA STATEMENT
I certify that this is my true and correct signature:

_____   _____
Borrower   Sample Signature

AKA STATEMENT
I further certify that I am also known as:

_____   _____
Name Variation (Print)   Sample Signature (Variation)

_____   _____
Name Variation (Print)   Sample Signature (Variation)

_____   _____
Name Variation (Print)   Sample Signature (Variation)

Figure 11:16 Sample Signature Affidavit

CLOSING VALIDATION

Please acknowledge receipt of all enclosures and your complete understanding of our instructions and conditions by signing and returning the instructions.

Closing Agent Acknowledgement: _____ Date: _____

_____

_____   _____

_____   _____

_____   _____

Please forward final Title Policy and Recorded Deed of Trust to:

Figure 11:17 Sample Closing Validation

UNIFORM RESIDENTIAL APPRAISAL REPORT

You are advised that you have the right, under the Equal Credit Opportunity Act, to obtain a copy of your Uniform Residential Appraisal Report.

If you wish a copy, please write us at the address shown below. We must hear from you no later than 90 days after we notify you about the action taken on your credit application or you withdraw your application.

Please send your written request to:

In your letter, give the following information:

       Loan or application number (if known)

       Date of application

       Name(s) of loan applicant(s)

       Property address

       Current mailing address

A copy of your Uniform Residential Appraisal Report shall be mailed to you within 30 days after receipt of your request.

Figure 11:18 Sample Appraisal Notice

FEE DISCLOSURE

APPLICANT(S) NAME AND ADDRESS	MORTGAGE BANKER/BROKER NAME AND ADDRESS
PROPERTY ADDRESS	TYPE OF LOAN

Today you have submitted a mortgage loan application to the Mortgage Banker or Broker listed above. All fees paid by you are nonrefundable. State law ( ) requires that the following information be disclosed to you.

The Mortgage Banker or Broker is required to refund all fees paid by an applicant borrower, other than those fees paid by the Mortgage Banker or Broker to a third party, when a mortgage loan is not produced within the time specified by the Mortgage Banker or Broker at the rate, term and overall cost agreed to by the borrower.

However, this provision shall not apply when the failure to produce a loan is due solely to the borrower's negligence, borrower's refusal to accept and close on a loan commitment or borrower's refusal or inability to provide information necessary for processing the loan, including, but not limited to, employment verifications and verifications of deposit.

This disclosure does not constitute approval of your loan or a commitment to make a loan to you.

Figure 11:19 Sample Fee Disclosure

OCCUPANCY DECLARATION

Lender:

RE: LOAN NO:

        PROPERTY ADDRESS

The undersigned Borrower of the above described property does hereby declare, under penalty of perjury as follows:

1.   Borrower shall occupy, establish and use the Property as Borrower principal residence within sixty days after execution of the Security Instrument and shall continue to occupy the Property as Borrower's principal residence for at least one year after the date of occupancy unless Lender otherwise agrees in writing, which consent shall not be unreasonably withheld, or unless extenuating circumstances exist which are beyond the Borrower's control.

        You are hereby informed that the Lender from time to time makes spot checks for owner occupancy on properties upon which we have secured a mortgage.

        Between the first and thirteenth day, after close of escrow, occupancy may be checked more than once. If after this check Lender is to believe that you never intended to occupy the subject as your primary residence, we may choose to call your note due and payable or increase your note rate by 100 basis points, in accordance with the applicable sections itemized on your note and Security Instrument and allowable by law.

2.   Borrower shall be in default, if during the loan application process, gave materially false or inaccurate information or statements to Lender (or failed to provide Lender with any material information) in connection with the loan evidenced by the Note, including but not limited to, representations concerning Borrower's occupancy of the Property as a Principal residence.

3.   The Lender has the right to foreclose on the loan under the terms of the Security Instrument if items 1 or 2 above are violated.

4.   Should Borrower's intention change prior to close transaction, then it is agreed that Lender will immediately be notified of that fact.

5.   Borrower understands that without this declaration of intention, Lender may not make the loan in connection with the property.

Figure 11:20 Sample Occupancy Declaration

CERTIFICATIONS, DISCLOSURES AND NOTICES

Name(s) / Address(es) of Applicant(s):

Property Address

OCCUPANCY CERTIFICATION

The above-described applicants, as evidenced by their signatures below, certify that, upon taking (or in case of a refinance, retaining) title to the above property, their occupancy status will be:

___ Primary Residence. Occupied by owner as his / her primary residence.

___ Secondary Residence. Occupied by owner as second home, while maintaining a principal residence elsewhere.

___ Investment Property. Not owner occupied. Purchased as an investment to be held or rented.

EMPLOYMENT CERTIFICATION

Information about an applicant's employment, income, and obligations is critical to determining whether or not an application for a loan will be approved. At the time of loan closing, applicants are required to execute a sworn statement that the information supplied on the loan application about employment and income is still current, and that the applicant has not received not of, or have knowledge of an impending layoff, and that the outstanding obligations of the applicant are still substantially the same as reported on the application. If there is a change in your employment or financial circumstances prior to loan closing, you must immediately notify your loan officer in order to obtain approval of the changes.

EQUAL CREDIT OPPORTUNITY ACT

The Federal Equal Credit Opportunity Act prohibits creditors from discriminating against credit applicants on the basis of race, color, religion, national origin, sex, marital status, age (provided the applicant has the capacity to enter into a binding contract); because all or a part of the applicant's income derives from any public assistance program; or because the applicant has in good faith exercised any right under the Consumer Credit Protection Act. The federal agency that administers compliance with this law concerning this creditor is:

FAIR CREDIT REPORTING ACT

The credit standing of all individual applicants for credit will be investigated, possibly by means of a consumer report from a consumer-reporting agency. The investigative consumer report may include information about an applicant's character, general reputation, personal characteristics, and mode of living, as applicable. As an applicant, you have the right to make a written request, within a reasonable period of time, for a disclosure of the nature and scope of the investigation. If you application for credit is denied due to an unfavorable consumer report, you will be notified of the identity of the Consumer Reporting Agency which furnished the report, and of your right to request, within sixty (60) days, the reasons for the adverse actions, as required by section 615(b) of the Fair Credit Reporting Act.

ANTI-COERSION STATEMENT

The insurance laws of the State provide that the Lender may not require the Borrower to take insurance through any particular insurance agent or company to protect the mortgaged property. The Borrower, subject to the rules adopted by the Insurance Commissioner, has the right to have the insurance placed with an Insurance Agency or Company of his or her choice, provided such Agency meets the requirements of the Lender. The Lender, however, has the right to designate reasonable financial and experience requirements as to the Company and the adequacy of the coverage.

If the selection of the Insurance Agent or Company is not mutually agreeable, then the Lender shall furnish the Borrower a copy of the Rules and Regulations promulgated by the Insurance Commissioner governing the placing of such insurance.

Applicant acknowledges having read the foregoing statement or the Rules of Insurance

Commissioner relative thereto, and understands applicant's rights and privileges and those of the Lender relative to the placing of such insurance. Applicant has selected the following entities to write the insurance covering the property described above:

Insurance Company:

Agent:

Agent's Address:

Agent's Telephone Number:

GOVERNMENT LOANS ONLY

Right to Financial Privacy Act of 1978 – The Department of Housing and Urban Development and/or the Department of Veterans Affairs has the right to access financial information held by a financial institution in determining whether to qualify an applicant as a prospective mortgagor under its program requirements. Financial records regarding your transaction will be available to the Department of Housing and Urban Development and / or the Department of Veterans Affairs without further notice or authorization, but it will not be disclosed or released outside the agency except as required or permitted by law.

ACKNOWLEDGEMENT

The applicant(s) identified above certify that he/she/they have read and understand the Disclosures, Notices and Certification above, as evidenced by his/her/their signature(s) below.

Figure 11:21 Sample Certification and Disclosure

Mortgage Servicing Disclosure

NOTICE TO MORTGAGE LOAN APPLICATNS: THE RIGHT TO COLLECT YOUR MORTGAGE LOAN PAYMENTS MAY BE TRANSFERRED. FEDERAL LAW GIVES YOU CERTAIN RELATED RIGHTS. READ THIS STATEMTN AND SIGN IT ONLY IF YOU UNDERSTAND ITS CONTENTS.

Because you are applying for a mortgage loan covered by the Real Estate Settlement Procedures Act (RESPA), you have certain rights under that Federal law. This statement tells you about those rights. It also tells you what the chances are that the servicing for this loan may be transferred to a different loan servicer. "Servicing" refers to collecting your principal, interest and escrow account payments, if any. If your loan servicer changes, certain procedures must be followed. This statement generally explains those procedures.

Transfer Practices and Requirements

If the servicing of your loan is assigned, sold or transferred to a new servicer you must be given notice of that transfer. The present loan servicer must send you notice in writing of the assignment, sale, or transfer of the servicing not less than 15 days before the effective date of the transfer. The present servicer and the new servicer may combine this information in one notice so long as the notice is sent to you within 15 days before the effective date of the transfer. The 15-day period is not applicable if a notice of prospective transfer is provided to you at settlement. The law allows a delay in the time (not more than 30 days after a transfer) for servicers to notify you under certain limited circumstances, when your servicer is changed abruptly. This exception applies only if your servicer is fired for cause, is in bankruptcy proceedings, or is involved in a conservatorship or receivership initiated by a Federal Agency.

Notices must contain certain information. They must contain the effective date of the transfer of the servicing of your loan to the new servicer, the name, address and toll-free or collect call telephone number of the new servicer, and toll-free or collect call telephone numbers of a person or department for both your present servicer and your new servicer to answer your questions about the transfer of servicing. During the 60-day period following the effective date of the transfer of the loan servicing, a loan payment received by your old servicer before its due date may not be treated by the new servicer as late and a late fee may not be imposed on you.

Complaint Resolution

Section 5 of RESPA gives you certain consumer rights *whether or not your loan servicing is transferred*. If you send a qualified written request to your loan servicer concerning the servicing of your loan, your servicer must provide you with a written acknowledgement within 20 business days of receipt of your request. A "qualified written request" is a written correspondence other than notice on payment coupon or other payment medium supplied by the servicer that includes your name and account number and your reasons for the request. Not later than 60 Business Days after receiving your request, your servicer must make any appropriate corrections to your account or must provide you with a written clarification regarding any dispute. During this 60-Business Day period, your servicer may not provide any information to a consumer reporting agency concerning any overdue payment related to such period or qualified written request.

A business day is any day excluding public holidays, State or Federal, Saturday or Sunday.

Damages and Costs

Section 6 of RESPA also provides for damages and costs for individuals in circumstances where servicers are shown to have violated the requirements of that section.

Servicing Transfer Estimated by Lender

1.   The following is the best estimate of what will happen to the servicing of your loan:

        We may assign, sell, or transfer the servicing of your loan sometime while the loan is outstanding. We are able to service your loan and we presently intend to service your loan.

2.   For all mortgage loans that we make in the 12-month period after your mortgage loan   is funded, we estimate that the percentage of mortgage loans for which we will transfer   servicing is between:

        ___ and ___%

        This is only our best estimate and it is not binding. Business conditions or other circumstances may affect

3.   This is our record of transferring the servicing of mortgage loans we have made in the past:

        Year   Percentage of Loans Transferred

ACKNOWLEDGEMENT OF MORTGAGE LOAN APPLICANT

I/We have read this disclosure form and understand the contents as evidenced by my/our signature(s) below. I/We understand that this acknowledgement is a required part of the mortgage loan application.

Figure 11:22 Sample Servicing Disclosure

NOTICE OF POSSIBLE TRANSFER OF LOAN
SERVICING ACCOUNT

Loan No.:

Borrower(s):

In the event _____ transfers the servicing of your loan to another Servicing Agent, you will be notified in writing by _____ and the new Servicing Agent.

The written information you will receive to notify you of a transfer would include:

(1)   The name and address of the Company to which the transfer of the servicing of   the indebtedness is made.

(2)   The date the transfer was or will be completed.

(3)   The address where all future payments are to be made and the due date of the next payment.

I/We hereby acknowledge I/we have received and read this Notice.

Figure 11:23 Sample Servicing Disclosure 2

F. Type of Loan			
1__ FHA 2 __ FmHA 3__ Conv 4 __ VA 5 __ Conv Ins	6. File Number:	7. Loan Number:	8. Mortgage Insurance Case Number

G.Note: This form is furnished to give you a statement of actual settlement costs. Amounts paid to and by the settlement agent are shown. Items marked "(P&C)" were paid outside the closing; they are shown here for informational purposes and are not included in the totals.

D. Name & Address of Borrower.	E. Name & Address of Seller	F. Name & Address of Lender
G. Property Location	H. Settlement Agent	I. Settlement Date
	Place of Settlement:	

J. Summary of Borrower's Transaction		**K. Summary of Seller's Transaction**	
100. Gross Amount Due From Borrower		**400. Gross Amount Due To Seller**	
101. Contract Sales Price		401. Contact Sales Price	
102. Personal Property		402. Personal Property	
103. Settlement Charges to borrower (line 1400)		403.	
104.		404.	
105.		405.	
Adjustments for items paid by seller in advance		Adjustments for items paid by seller in advance	
106. City / Town Taxes for		406. City / Town Taxes for	
107. County Taxes for		407. County Taxes for	
108. Assessments for		408. Assessments for	
109.		409.	
110.		410.	
111.		411.	
112.		412.	
120. Gross Amount Due From Borrower		**420. Gross Amount Due To Seller**	
200. Amounts Paid By Or In Behalf Of Borrower		**500. Reductions In Amount Due To Seller**	
201. Deposit or earnest money		501. Excess deposit (see instructions)	
202. Principal amount of new loan(s)		502. Settlement charges to seller (line 1400)	
203. Existing loan(s) take subject to		503. Existing loan(s) taken subject to	
204.		504. Payoff of first mortgage loan	
205.		505. Pay off of second mortgage loan	
206.		506.	
207.		507.	
208.		508.	
209.		509.	
Adjustments for items unpaid by seller		**Adjustments for items unpaid by seller**	
210. City / Town Taxes for		510. City / Town Taxes for	
211. County Taxes for		511. County Taxes for	
212. Assessments for		512. Assessments for	
213.		513.	
214.		514.	
215.		515.	
216.		516.	
217.		517.	
218.		518.	
219.		519.	
220. Total Paid By/For Borrower		**520. Total Reduction Amount Due Seller**	
300. Cash At Settlement From/To Borrower		**600. Cash at Settlement To/From Seller**	
301. Gross amount due from borrower (line 120)		601. Gross amount due to seller (line 420)	
302. Less amounts paid by/for borrower (line 220)	( )	602. Less reductions in amt due seller (line 520)	( )

Figure 13:2 Sample HUD Page 1

	Paid From Borrowers Funds at Settlement	Paid From Seller's Funds at Settlement
700. Total Sales/Brokers commission based on price $ @ %		
Division of Commission (line 700) as follows:		
701. $ to		
702. $ to		
703 Commission paid at Settlement		
704.		
800. Items Payable in Connection with Loan		
801. Loan Origination Fee %		
802. Loan Discount %		
803. Appraisal Fee to		
804. Credit Report to		
805. Lender's Inspection Fee		
806. Mortgage Insurance Application Fee to		
807. Assumption Fee		
808.		
809.		
810.		
900. Items Required By Lender To Be Paid In Advance		
901. Interest from to @$ / day		
902. Mortgage Insurance Premium for months to		
903. Hazard Insurance Premium for years to		
904.		
905.		
1000. Reserves Deposited With Lender		
1001. Hazard Insurance months @$ per month		
1002. Mortgage Insurance months @$ per month		
1003. City Property Taxes months @$ per month		
1004. County Property Taxes months @$ per month		
1005. Annual Assessments months @$ per month		
1006. months @$ per month		
1007. months @$ per month		
1008. months @$ per month		
1100. Title Charges		
1101. Settlement or closing fee to		
1102. Abstract or title search to		
1103. Title examination to		
1104. Title insurance binder to		
1105. Document preparation to		
1106. Notary fees to		
1107. Attorney's fees to		
(includes above items numbers:)		
1108. Title Insurance to		
(includes above items numbers:)		
1109. Lender's coverage $		
1110. Owner's coverage $		
1111.		
1112.		
1200. Government Recording and Transfer Charges		
1201. Recording fees: Deed $: Mortgage $: Releases $		
1202. City/county tax/stamps: Deed $: Mortgage $		
1203. State tax/stamps: Deed $: Mortgage $		
1204.		
1205.		
1300. Additional Settlement Charges		
1301. Survey to		
1302. Pest Inspection to		
1400. Total Settlement Charges (enter on lines 103, Section J and 502, Section K)		

Title Company Disclosure Form

Title Company File No.

RE:

Property Address:

This, the day _____ of _____, 20____, came _____
known as Borrower/Buyer and_____Seller (fill in Seller's
name, if this is a Sale of the Property), and acknowledged receipt and disclosure of the
following items. Said party(s) also acknowledge that _____ in
and for the State of _____ ("know collectively as "COMPANY" or "TITLE
COMPANY") is relying on the foregoing, and without such acknowledgement, the said
COMPANY would not issue its Policy(s) of Title Insurance.

INSTRUCTIONS for completing this form:

If this is a Refinance, Borrower INITIAL 3s 1, 3a, 5, 6, 7, 8, 10, and 11

If this is a Purchase, both Borrower and Seller to INITIAL where appropriate.

Figure 13:3 Sample Title Company Disclosure Page 1

Seller's Initials	Borrower's Initials	1.) AFFIDAVIT OF DEBTS AND LIENS. Borrower and Seller each acknowledge that there are no other liens, judgments or other involuntary liens served, filed or recorded against said parties, and that effect the Real Property, that is not already disclosed, the parties swear and/or affirm the following as current liens or judgments effecting the real property. (if none, write "none"):
	Borrower's Initials	2.) WAIVER OF INCPECTION. Since examines only the record title and does not actually see the property, we hereby waive inspection by of this property and accept our policy subject to the rights of parties in possession. We agree that it is our responsibility to inspect said premises and to obtain possession of it from the present occupants, if any.
Seller's Initials	Borrower's Initials	3. (A) ACCPETANCE OF SURVEY. Borrower has received and reviewed a copy of the survey, if any, of the Property made in connection with this transaction and acknowledges being aware of the following matters of encroachment, protrusion, conflict, or discrepancy disclosed by the survey. If there is no survey, you affirm that there have been no changes to the property since the day of the last survey that would trigger encroachments or protrusions over dedicated easements or building setback lines. If you do not know the answer to this question, write on the spaces below, any improvements to the property, e.g. swimming pools, additions to the home, gazebos or other structures, whether temporary or permanent that are not won the property since you became Owner. DO NOT indicate new Landscaping. NOTE ALSO: That the transaction may involve NEW CONSTRUCTION, for which no survey is yet prepared at the time of closing. The Borrower's herein acknowledge they are responsible to provide a FINAL SURVEY to the "Company" after completion and acceptance of the construction. Any final Policy of Title Insurance will be subject to those matters shown within such FINAL SURVEY.

	Borrower's Initials	3. (B) BOUNDARY COVERAGE. As proposed to be issued, Borrower's Owner Policy will contain a general exception to any discrepancies or conflicts in area or Boundary lines, and any encroachments, protrusions, or overlapping of improvements. ON payment of an additional Owners Policy premium, policy coverage against these matters is available subject to TITLE COMPANY'S approval of a current survey of the Property and without limiting specific exceptions to matters disclosed by the survey. If you want the additional coverage and this is a Purchase, so indicate by writing YES:
Seller's Initials	Borrower's Initials	4.) PROPERTY TAX PRORATIONS. Property taxes for the current year have been prorated between BUYER and SELLER, who each acknowledge and understand that these prorations are based upon (a) the sales price or the most current appraised value available and the most current tax rate available or (b) some other common method of estimation. SELLER warrants and represents that there are no past due taxes owed on the Property and if such warranty and representation is untrue the SELLER shall reimburse the Title Company, on demand, for any sums paid by the Title Company to pay such taxes, and any related penalty and interest. BUYER and SELLER each agree that when amounts of the current year's taxes become known and payable they will adjust any changes of the proration and reimbursement between themselves and that TITLE COMPANY shall have no liability or obligation with respect to these prorations.
	Borrower's Initials	5.) TAX RENDITION AND EXEMPTIONS. Although the Central Appraiser District (CAD) may independently determine Borrower's new ownership and billing address, BUYER is still obligated by law to "render" the Property for taxation by notifying the CAD of the changes in the Property's ownership and of BORROWER'S proper address for tax billing. BUYER is advised that current year's taxes may have been assessed on the basis of various exemptions obtained by SELLER (e.g., homestead or over 65).

		It is the BORROWER'S responsibility to qualify for BORROWER'S own tax exemptions and to meet any requirements prescribed by the taxing authorities. BUYER Acknowledges and understands these obligations and the fact that TITLE COMPANY assumes no responsibility for accuracy of CAD records concerning ownership, tax-billing address, or status of exemptions.
	Borrower's Initials	6.) HOMEOWNER'S ASSOCIATION. Buyer acknowledges that ownership of the PROPERTY involves membership in a homeowner's association. BORROWER is responsible for contacting the homeowner's association immediate to asce3rtain the exact amount of future dues or assessments. TITLE COMPANY has made no representations with respect to, such Association's annual budget, pending repairs or deferred maintenance, if any, or other debts of the association. BUYER accepts sole responsibility to obtain such information and verify its accuracy to BORROWER'S satisfaction. IF THERE IS NO HOMEOWNER'S ASSOCIATION – PLEASE DISREGARD.
Seller's Initials	Borrower's Initials	7.) CLOSING DISCLAIMER. SELLER and BORROWER ach acknowledge and understand that the above referenced transaction has not yet "closed". Any change in possession of the Property takes place AT BORROWER'S AND SELLER'S OWN RISK. THIS TRANSACTION IS NOT CLOSED UNTIL: A) ALL TITLE REQUIREMENTS ARE COMPLETED TO THE SATISFACTION OF TITLE COMPANY. B) ALL NECESSARY DOCUMETNS ARE PROPERLY EXECUTED, REVIEWED, AND ACCPETED BY THE PATRIES TO THIS TRANSACTION AND BY TITLE COMPANY; AND, C) ALL FUNDS ARE COLLECTED AND DELIVERED TO AND ACCEPTED BY THE PARTEIS TO WHOM THEY ARE DUE.

	Borrower's Initials	8.) ARBITRATION. Depending on the language of our Title Policy in your State, we may arbitrate any title disputes.
Seller's Initials		9.) IRS REPORTING. SELLER acknowledges having received at closing a copy of the HUD-1 Settlement Statement as a Substitute Form 1099-8. In accordance with federal tax regulations, information from the HUD-1 Statement will be furnished to the Internal Revenue Service.
Seller's Initials	Borrower's Initials	10.) ERRORS AND OMMISSIONS. In the event that any of the documents prepared in connection with the closing of this transaction contain errors which misstate or inaccurately reflect the true and correct terms, conditions and provisions of this closing, and the inaccuracy or misstatement is due to a clerical error or to a unilateral mistake on the part of the TITLE COMPANY, or to a mutual mistake on the part of the TITEL COMPANY AND/OR THE SELLER AND/OR THE BUYER, the undersigned agree to execute, in a timely manner, such correction documents as TITLE COMPANY may deem necessary to remedy such inaccuracy or misstatement.
	Borrower's Initials	11.) ATTORENY REPRESENTATION NOTICE. BUYER may wish to consult an attorney to discuss the matters shown on Schedule B or C of the Commitment for Title Insurance that was issued in connection with this transaction. The Title Insurance Policy will be a legal contract between BUYER and the underwriter. Neither the Commitment for Title Insurance nor the Title Insurance Policy are abstracts of title, title reports, or representations of title. They are contracts of indemnity. No representation is made that your intended use of the Property is allowed under law or under the restrictions or exceptions affecting the Property.

Figure 13:4   Sample Title Company Disclosure

RE: Escrow No.

PROCEEDS AUTHORIZTION

Buyer(s):

Property Address:

1.   One check payable to _____

     Mailed to this address_____

     _____

     a.   Regular Mail
     b.   Overnight Mail
     c.   Overnight Mail with Release Signature

2.   Wired to this account (I understand there is a $15 Fee)

     ABA Routing No._____

     Bank Name _____

     Name on Account _____

     Account No. _____

Figure 13:5 Sample Proceeds Authorization

CERTIFICATE OF RECORDATION OF DOCUMENTS

LENDER:

The undersigned hereby certifies that all documents that necessitate recordation in connection with that certain loan made by the above Lender to

Mortgagor, have been sent for recording to the Office of the Clerk of the Circuit Court of the county or city wherein the property lies.

Executed this day of:

Figure 14:1 Sample Certificate of Recordation

www.ingramcontent.com/pod-product-compliance
Lightning Source LLC
Chambersburg PA
CBHW082357270326
41935CB00013B/1657